Archæological Handbook

OF THE

COUNTY OF GLOUCESTER.

BY

G. B. WITTS, C.E.

BEING AN

EXPLANATORY DESCRIPTION

OF THE

Archæological Map of Gloucestershire,

By the same Author,

On which are shown 113 Ancient Camps, 26 Roman Villas, 40 Long Barrows, 126 Round Barrows, and a large number of British and Roman Roads.

PREFACE.

The object of this work is to place before Antiquaries, and all who are interested in the county of Gloucester, a short description of the numerous Ancient Camps, Roman Villas, Barrows, British Trackways, and Roman Roads to be found in every part of the County.

Hitherto, any one wishing for information on these subjects has been obliged to refer to numerous rare volumes and transactions of learned societies not easily to be obtained ; and even then they might not find what they require, as many of the antiquities herein described have not been noticed in print before. It is hoped that the plan adopted of giving, in a condensed form, a description of each subject, will prove sufficient for the ordinary observer, while the references to the volumes and pages of those works that have previously mentioned it, will be found useful in directing to the proper source those who wish for fuller information. The writer has endeavoured to carry out the following excellent piece of advice, viz.—" that the author of a handbook on Archæology should, above all things, eschew fine writing and confine himself to matters of fact." Thus, he has preferred speaking of " Ancient " Camps, instead of classing them as "British," "Roman," and "post-Roman;" if this had not been done, facts would have given way to suppositions, and, once the door of imagination is opened to the antiquary, there seems little chance of controlling the impetuosity of his upward flight! As a matter of fact, the writer agrees with Mr. BAKER's opinion, as given in the "Archæologia," that nearly all the Ancient Camps of Gloucestershire were originally constructed by the British. Many of them, doubtless, were much altered by the Romans, and some—especially that at Sodbury—seem to be decidedly Roman in character.

The writer cannot indulge the hope that the following is a complete list of the British and Roman antiquities of Gloucestershire, as no doubt many yet remain undiscovered beneath the sod. The number of Roman Villas, especially, may be expected to increase considerably as years roll on.

In concluding this short Introduction, the writer begs to express his sincere thanks to all those who have so kindly assisted him by giving information from all parts of the county, and trusts that when fresh antiquities are discovered he may be favoured with a repetition of their kindness.

immediately above the village of Amberley, and one mile north of Nailsworth. It is formed by a slight mound and ditch, which had probably a stockade on the top, running on a curved line from the village of Littleworth to the escarpment above Spriggswell, enclosing an area of about 50 acres. A very strong line of earthworks is constructed across this area, dividing it into two parts, and a slight mound connects the camp with the much larger one of Minchinhampton. Mr. Playne says there are upwards of 700 ancient pit dwellings in close proximity, some inside and some outside the camp, but most numerous near the escarpment.

See Rudder's "History of Gloucestershire," p. 468.
Also "Proceedings Cott. Nat. Field Club," vol. v., p. 285.
Also Fosbrooke's "History of Gloucestershire," vol. i., p. 376.
Also Bigland's "History of Gloucestershire," vol. ii., p. 6.

No. 5.—BAGENDON EARTHWORKS, No. 1.

In the parish of Bagendon, three miles north of Cirencester, extensive earthworks are still to be seen. They were visited by the members of the Cotteswold Naturalists' Field Club in May, 1881, and from the enormous extent of the works they appear to have been rather the boundary line of some pre-historic tribe than for purposes of defence. There is a double line of earthworks, with a space of about 100 yards between them. They commence in a plantation on the hill above the Bear Inn at Perrott's Brook, and extend in a northerly direction across the marshy ground near the Churn. The inner line then ascends the hill by the side of Cutham Lane. The outer line has been nearly destroyed, but can be traced in the fields. The works are seen again close to the grounds of North Cerney House, at which point they turn towards the west by Scrubditch Farm, extending for more than one and a half miles.

See Rudder's "History of Gloucestershire," p. 258.
Also "Proceedings Cott. Nat. Field Club," vol. vi., p. 212.

No. 6.—BAGENDON EARTHWORKS, No. 2.

There is another line of entrenchments half a mile east of the river Churn, directly facing the foregoing. They consist of earthworks, with the ditch on the western side of the mound, whereas the ditches of the Bagendon Work, No. 1, are on the eastern side. It thus appears probable that these two series of earthworks were constructed by opposing forces.

See " Proceedings Cott. Nat. Field Club," vol. vi., p. 212.

No. 7.—BATSFORD CAMP.

This camp lies within half a mile of the town of Moreton-in-the-Marsh, though it is in the parish of Batsford, close to the Roman station of Dorn and the ancient Fosse Way. It is nearly rectangular in shape, and measures 70 yards by 60 yards. The earthworks consist of a single mound and ditch, measuring in some places 5 feet from the bottom of the ditch to the top of the mound. The road from Moreton to Batsford cuts through the centre of the entrenchments. A large number of Roman coins and other antiquities have been found in the neighbourhood.

See Rudder's "History of Gloucestershire," p. 265.

No. 8.—BEACHLEY BULWARKS.

These were situated on rising ground at Beachley Green, one and a half miles south-east of Chepstow, near the banks of the river Severn. Rudder mentions earthworks existing there in his day, but no traces are now to be seen of them, though two fields lying on the slope, between the high ground and the river Wye, are still known as the "Upper and Lower Bulwarks."

See Rudder's " History of Gloucestershire," p. 762.
Also " Proceedings Cott. Nat. Field Club," vol. vi., p. 239.

No. 9.—BECKBURY CAMP.

This stands on a projecting point of the Cotswold Hills, above Hayles Wood, in the hamlet of Farmcote, two and a half miles north-east of Winchcomb. It is defended by a considerable entrenchment, somewhat irregular in form, resting on the steep escarpment of the hill at each end. The bank is nearly 300 yards in length, and the area defended about 4 acres. It commands a most extensive prospect over the surrounding country, and from it can be seen no less than twelve other fortified positions. There is a spring of water outside the entrenchments, at the north-west angle, and apparently there was a covered approach leading down to it.

See "Proceedings Cott. Nat. Field Club," vol. iv., p. 207.

No. 10.—BIGSWEAR ENTRENCHMENTS.

This is marked on the Ordnance Map as an "Ancient Entrenchment." It lies in the parish of St. Briavel's, one mile west of the village, and close to the river Wye. Mr. Playne says, "The position is well suited for defence, the headland having a steep bank round it; but there are no traces of entrenchments left." From a recent examination of the ground, I think it very probable that the entrenchment referred to on the Ordnance Map is part of Offa's Dyke, which runs through St. Margaret's Grove just to the east of Bigswear Bridge.

See "Proceedings Cott. Nat. Field Club," vol. vi., p. 236.

No. 11.—BIRDLIP CAMP.

This occupies a projecting ridge of the Cotswolds on Birdlip Hill, in the parish of Cowley, half a mile north of the village of Birdlip, four and a half miles south of Cheltenham. The present area is one acre, defended by a mound and ditch running on a curved line, with each end resting on the escarpment. Originally this camp must have been larger, the quarrying operations having interfered with the extent of the defended area, and the mounds being nearly obliterated by the action of the plough. A great number of flint arrow-heads have been found in the immediate neighbourhood.

See "Proceedings Cott. Nat. Field Club," vol. vi., p. 210.
Also "Transactions Bristol and Glou. Archæ. Soc.," 1879-80, p. 206.

ANCIENT CAMPS.

No. 12.—Bitton Camp.

This is in the parish of Bitton, close to the village, and five miles north-west of Bath. It lies just to the north of the celebrated Roman road that ran from Aquæ Sulis to Venta Silurum, and is mentioned in the "Itinerary" of Antonine, where it is called Trajectus. There has been considerable discussion on this point, but the most probable solution is that given by Bishop Clifford. (See Trajectus.)

The camp was square in form, and measured about 100 yards in each direction; the earthworks, however, that formed the defences of the camp have long since been disturbed and mutilated. A large number of other Roman remains have been found in the parish of Bitton at various times, including four Roman villas.

See "Proceedings Cott. Nat. Field Club," vol. vi., p. 231.
Also "The History of the Parish of Bitton," by the Rev. H. T. Ellacombe, F.S.A.
Also "Transactions Bristol and Glou. Archæ. Soc.," 1878-79, p. 88.

No. 13.—Blackenbury Camp.

This stands on Westridge Hill, in the parish of Wotton-under-Edge, and two miles south of Dursley. It consists of two banks and a ditch, running across a promontory of the Cotswold Hills, having an entrance at each end. The area enclosed is eight acres, and the measurement along the mound is about 800 yards. Rudder says this was called "Becket's Bury." Scattered all over the plateau of Westridge, adjacent to the camp, were found innumerable pit dwellings. Some of them were very large, being from 20 to 30 feet in diameter, and seven feet deep. Upwards of 600 small pits have been counted in the immediate vicinity, but, although they were found close up to the entrenchments of the camp, not one has been observed within the fortified area.

See Rudder's "History of Gloucestershire," p. 847.
Also "Archæologia," vol. xix., p. 166.
Also "Proceedings Cott. Nat. Field Club," vol. vi., p. 217.

ANCIENT CAMPS.

No. 14.—BLAIZE CASTLE.

This stands on a high conical hill in the parish of Henbury, four miles north-west of Bristol, a little to the north of the Roman station Abone. The south side of the hill is very steep, and on the other sides the camp was defended by two banks and ditches, now invisible. An old paved road, called the "Fosse way," is observable running up the north-east side of the hill, at the top of which is an entrance into the camp. There is another entrance in the direction of King's Weston Hill. The position is naturally a very strong one, from the steepness of the hillsides both on the east, west, and south. The shape is irregular, and the area defended is six acres. In 1766, some brass coins of Vespasian, Antoninus, Constantine, Constantius, Tetricus, and others of the later Empire were found here, with a few silver ones, chiefly of Gordianus.

See Atkyn's "History of Gloucestershire," p. 248 (with plate).
Also Rudder's "History of Gloucestershire," p. 491.
Also "Archæologia," vol. xix., p. 162.
Also "Proceedings Cott. Nat. Field Club," vol. vi., p. 231.

No. 15.—BLISBURY CAMP.

The top of Blisbury Hill, in the parish of Berkeley, three miles south-west of the town, is supposed to have been fortified, though the remains of the earthworks are now very slight. Mr. Playne says, "An area of rather more than an acre in extent, and oval in form, has been defended by having the already steep sides of the hill scarped so as to form a steeper bank, six or eight feet high. To this enclosed area there is an entrance protected by mounds." There are extensive views from this position.

See "Proceedings Cott. Nat. Field Club," vol. vi., p. 228.

No. 16.—BLOODY ACRE CAMP.

This is a remarkably fine camp, and one of the most perfect in the county. It is situated on an eminence known as the "Camp Hill," in Tortworth Park, in the parish of Cromhall, three-quarters of a mile north of the village. The narrow top of the hill is nearly level, the eastern side being very steep, almost precipitous. On the north side there are two banks and ditches, running across the hill top. On the south-west side there are three banks and ditches, and here they have a very fine appearance, with the mounds increasing in height and strength one behind the other. The outer line measures ten feet from the bottom of the ditch to the top of the mound, the second line fifteen feet, and the third line twenty feet.

See "Archæologia," vol. xix., p. 164.
Also Rudder's History of Gloucestershire," p. 397.
Also " Proceedings Cott. Nat. Field Club," vol. iv., p. 22.
Also "Proceedings Cott. Nat. Field Club," vol. vi., p. 229.

No. 17.—Bredon Camp, No. 1.

On the highest part of Bredon Hill, in the parish of Kemerton, and three miles north-east of the village of Bredon, is a fine camp, formed on the precipitous brow of the hill by two lines of entrenchments, which run on a curve, with each end resting on the edge of the escarpment. The outer line is about 100 yards from the inner. Both have deep ditches and high mounds, the top of the mounds in some parts being still 20 feet from the bottom of the ditch. Large numbers of Roman coins have been found here, and I have also found many flint chips, cores, and worked flakes in the immediate vicinity. Inside the camp, on the brow of the escarpment, is a hollow place, in which lies a mass of stone known as the "Bambury Stone." A landslip on the north side of this camp took place about sixty years back, which disclosed a quantity of charred corn that had been stored in a cavity, probably for the use of the occupiers of the camp.

See Rudder's "History of Gloucestershire," p. 506.
Also " Archæologia," vol. xix., p. 172.
Also " Proceedings Cott. Nat. Field Club," vol vi., p. 224.

No. 18.—BREDON CAMP, No. 2.

This camp is also on Bredon Hill, three-quarters of a mile north of the village of Conderton, and one and a half from Beckford. It is in the county of Worcester, though only a few hundred yards from the boundary of our county. It is irregular in shape, though somewhat approaching an oval in form. Its position is remarkable, as it is placed on a sloping promontory on the south side of the hill, some 200 or 300 feet below the summit. Small valleys run on each side of the camp, and the space between them has been fortified by a single ditch and mound on three sides, and, as an additional defence, the steep slope has been artificially scarped. On the south side the camp has a double line of earthworks, the distance between them being 40 yards. There is an entrance on the north side, leading towards the top of Bredon Hill. The land on each side of the adjoining valleys is on the same level as the camp, and there are some fine springs of water just outside the fortifications. The camp commands a grand view of the range of the Cotswold Hills, and of the Severn valley towards Cheltenham and Gloucester.

See Nash's " History of Worcestershire."

No. 19.—BURY CAMP.

This camp is in Wiltshire, being one mile outside the boundary of our county. It lies two miles east of Marshfield, and two miles north of Colerne, on the point of a hill, with the sides flanked by valleys, and it is defended by earthworks running across the hill top from valley to valley. The area defended is about 25 acres.

See " Proceedings Cott. Nat. Field Club," vol. vi., p. 222.

No. 20.—BURYHILL CAMP.

This is to be found on Bury Hill, in the parish of Mangotsfield, one mile from Winterbourne, and two miles north-west of Mangotsfield. It has two banks, and a ditch between them. It is irregular in form, about 200 yards long and 100 yards wide. There is an entrance on the south side. Rudder mentions another camp, in the parish of Winterbourne, not far from this.

See Rudder's " History of Gloucestershire," p. 536.
Also " Archæologia," vol. xix., p. 161.
Also "Proceedings Cott. Nat. Field Club," vol. vi., p. 231.

No. 21.—CAERWOOD CAMP.

This is in the parish of Tidenham, on a peninsular formed by the river Wye, on which the Chapelry of Llancaut is situate, two miles north of Chepstow. This has been claimed as part of Offa's Dyke ; but, from a careful examination of the ground in July, 1881, I found that the earthworks were very different in character to that celebrated boundary, and I agree with Mr. G. F. Playne, that this was a distinct fortified position, though some of the entrenchments may have been utilised by Offa. The peninsular is cut off from the mainland by earthworks, consisting chiefly of two banks and two ditches, each end of this line resting on the precipitous rocks which tower over the river Wye. At a distance of about 400 yards from the above is another defence, consisting of a mound six feet high and twenty feet wide at its base, also running across the hill top, with each end resting on the escarpment, the area thus defended being nearly twelve acres.

See " Proceedings Cott. Nat. Field Club," vol. vi., p. 237.

No. 22.—CAM LONG DOWN CAMP.

The hill called Cam Long Down stands in the parish of Cam, one mile north-east of Dursley, in advance of the Cotswold range, but only three-quarters of a mile to the west of Uley Bury. On the summit of this hill are signs of earthworks, though now very slight. There are also the remains of many ancient pit dwellings, and large quantities of worked flints have been found.

See " Proceedings Cott. Nat. Field Club," vol. vi., p. 227.

No. 23.—CHARLTON ABBOTS CAMP.

This is one of the few circular camps to be found in Gloucestershire. It lies three-quarters of a mile to the east of the village of Charlton Abbots, in the parish of Hawling, but close to the boundary. It is three miles south-east of Winchcomb. This camp is defended by a single mound and ditch, now much levelled by the action of the plough, though the line of the earthworks can still be clearly traced. The position is by no means a strong one, being nearly on a level with the surrounding ground. There seems to have been an entrance on the east side.

See "Proceedings Cott. Nat. Field Club," vol. vi., p. 209.
Also "Transactions Bristol and Glou. Archæ. Soc.," 1879-80, p. 206.

No. 24.—CHASTLETON CAMP.

This fine camp is in Oxfordshire, though only a few yards from the boundary of our county. It lies in the parish of Chastleton, four miles north-east of Stow-on-the-Wold. It is very nearly circular, and the area defended is close upon twelve acres. The mound is in some places still twelve feet high; there are no signs of a ditch, and probably there never was one. Entrances are still to be traced both on the east and west sides. Though this camp lies on high ground, it is not raised above the land in the immediate neighbourhood. A few miles to the north-east of this camp are the celebrated Rollwright stone circles, well worth a visit.

See "Proceedings Cott. Nat. Field Club," vol. vi., p. 223.

No. 25.—CHURCHDOWN CAMP.

It has often been suggested that there was an ancient camp on Churchdown Hill, three miles east of Gloucester, and, from its commanding position and great natural strength, there seems little doubt but that it was occupied at an early date, though I am unable to find any satisfactory traces of defensive earthworks. Viewed from the village of

Hucclecote, it has every appearance of a great fortress; but this is accounted for by the natural configuration of the soil Mr. Baker, in describing it in the "Archæologia," writes, "Its shape is very irregular, conforming entirely to that of the ground, and is rendered very imperfect by stone digging."

See "Archæologia," vol. xix., p. 169.
Also "Proceedings Cott. Nat. Field Club," vol. vi., p. 226.
Also "Transactions Bristol and Glou. Archæ. Soc.," 1879-80, p. 206.

No. 26.—CLEEVE HILL CAMP, No. 1.

This is a very interesting camp, in the parish of Cleeve, on the brow of the lofty Cotswold Hills, above the village of Prestbury, and three miles north-east of Cheltenham. A small area of four acres is protected by a very strong line of earthworks, consisting of two banks and two ditches, 350 yards in length, forming an irregular crescent, with each end resting on the precipitous escarpment of Cleeve Hill. There is a well-preserved entrance on the north side, where the earthworks are stronger than elsewhere. There are remains of four circular buildings attached to this camp, built with very thin stones without mortar—the diameter of the first building, which is just outside the camp on the south-east side, is 50 feet, the walls being three feet thick; the second building is within the camp, and is 53 feet in diameter; the third is outside the camp, on the north-west side, and, like the first, is 50 feet in diameter; the fourth building is further to the north, and is only ten feet in diameter. The foundations of a wall, several hundred yards in length, can be traced, enclosing all these buildings, and it extends to the edge of the precipice at each end. The situation of this fortress is remarkable, inasmuch as the ground rises far above the level of the camp towards the east; but there seem to have been watch-towers on the summit of the hill, traces of which can still be seen. A road leads out of the enclosure on the south side to the village of

ANCIENT CAMPS.

Prestbury, and in descending the hill this is sunk from ten to fifteen feet below the level of the adjoining lands.

> See Rudder's " History of Gloucestershire," p. 369.
> Also "Archæologia," vol. xix., p. 171.
> Also " Proceedings Cott. Nat. Field Club," vol. vi., p. 209.
> Also " Transactions Bristol and Glou. Archæ. Soc.," 1879-80, p. 204.
> Also Norman's " History of Cheltenham," p. 18.

No. 27.—CLEEVE HILL ENTRENCHMENTS.

These are in the parish of Cleeve, a little to the north of the camp just described. There is a line of earthworks, consisting of a single mound and ditch, running from the western escarpment of the hill for nearly a mile in a north-easterly direction, cutting off the northern portion of Cleeve Hill from the southern, at a point were one of the deep gullies runs down to Postlip. To the north of this line are two small circular earthworks of peculiar form, and it is difficult to say for what purpose they were intended. These works have not been previously described.

No. 28.—CLIFTON CAMP.

This crowned the highest point of the precipitous St. Vincent's Rocks, in the parish of Clifton, near Bristol. The defensive works were originally very regular and strong, there being three high mounds and three ditches, running on a curved line from the edges of the precipitous escarpment.

Within this strong fortification are some small mounds, suggesting a Roman occupation of an earlier work. William of Worcester, A.D. 1450, attributes this camp to one Ghyst, a giant. In his time large and small stones were placed round its circuit. Leman supposed that the Wans Dyke, which can be traced from the woodlands of Berkshire, terminated at this point. Its area is about two acres. Part of the works have been destroyed by making the approach to the Suspension Bridge, and the northern side has suffered in laying out public walks. This was known to the Britons as Caer Oder. Facing this camp, on the other side of the river Avon, are two strong camps in the Stokeleigh Woods.

> See " History and Antiquities of the City of Bristol," by W. Barrett.
> Also " Archæologia," vol. xix., p. 162.
> Also " Archæologia," vol. xliv., p. 428.
> Also Rudder's " History of Gloucestershire," p. 376.
> Also " History of Bristol," by Seyer.
> Also " Proceedings Cott. Nat. Field Club," vol. vi., p. 232.

No. 29.—Cold Aston Camp.

This was situated in the parish of Cold Aston, one mile to the north-east of the village, and one and a half miles from Bourton-on-the-Water. Rudder says, "In the camp-field, on the right hand of the road leading to Bourton-on-the-Water, are entrenchments now pretty much levelled, and a tumulus or barrow at a small distance from them which hath not been opened. I am informed that Roman coins have been found there, which indicate the works to be of that people, and probably served as an advanced post to their stronger fortification at Bourton." The tumulus is still in existence, but I can find no signs of the entrenchments. A great number of flint arrow-heads have been found here, and there is every probability that this position was occupied by the early inhabitants of our county. The camp mentioned at Bourton (see Salmonsbury) was certainly pre-Roman.

> See Rudder's " History of Gloucestershire," p. 238.
> Also " Transactions Bristol and Glou. Archæ. Soc.," 1879-80, p. 207.

No. 30.—Combesbury Camp.

This is situated in the parish of Tidenham, a little to the south-west of the church, and one and half miles from Chepstow. It is a small circular camp, enclosing an area of nearly one acre. The defence is slight, consisting of a single bank with a ditch outside. The bank seems to be chiefly composed of stones, and is strongest on the south side. This camp lies a little to the west of the Roman road leading from Glevum to Venta Silurum, and commands fine views over the river Severn, &c.

See "Proceedings Cott. Nat. Field Club," vol. vi., p. 236.

No. 31.—Condicote Camp.

This was a circular camp, situated in the parish of Condicote, close to the village, and three miles to the north-west of Stow-on-the-Wold. It was defended by a single mound and ditch, which is now nearly obliterated by the process of cultivation. Seventy years ago, however, the banks were so steep that it was difficult to climb to the top of them. The area enclosed is nearly four acres, the diameter of the circle being 160 yards. There is a good supply of water close at hand, and another camp of a striking character within half a mile (see Eubury Camp). On a recent visit to Condicote, I found a great number of worked flint flakes and chips, some of them inside the camp.

See "Proceedings Cott. Nat. Field Club," vol. vi., p. 208.

No. 32.—Cooper's Hill Camp.

The point of Cooper's Hill (two miles west of Birdlip and four and a half miles south-east of Gloucester) was evidently fortified, but, owing to landslips and quarries, most of the earthworks have disappeared.

In addition, however, to the point of the hill showing traces of fortifications, there appears to have been a very large camp extending due south, in the direction of Cranham, and having an area of nearly 200 acres. The earthworks protecting this area can still be traced in Cranham Woods. They consist of two mounds with a ditch between them, and in some places the principal mound is still 15 feet above the bottom of the ditch. Commencing on the edge of the escarpment, near Prinknash Park, these works run in an easterly direction for more than half a mile; they then cross the road leading from

Birdlip to Painswick, and turn to the north by Buckholt Cottage; and at this point they are particularly strong, the entrance to the enclosure being well preserved. They then continue in a northerly direction until they reach the escarpment above the Roman villa at Witcomb. For nearly half a mile after leaving Prinknash there is a second line, consisting of a single mound and ditch, running parallel to the main work and 40 yards from it. Due south of this large enclosure, which from its size and appearance must have been an extensive British settlement rather than a camp, was a small fortified position protecting its weakest point. This *place d'armes* is irregular in shape, having an area of about three-quarters of an acre.

The main earthworks described above were discovered by the writer in 1881, but the following authorities mention the entrenchments on the point of the hill.

See " Archæologia," vol. xix., p. 170.
Also " Proceedings Cott. Nat. Field Club," vol. vi., p. 211.
Also " Transactions Bristol and Glou. Archæ. Soc.," 1879-80, p. 206.

No. 33.—CORINIUM.

The British town Caer Cori (now Cirencester) was doubtless a fortified position, but the succeeding Roman town, Corinium, obliterated all traces of its earlier occupation. The earthworks defending the Roman town can still be traced, and measure no less than two and a quarter miles in circumference, showing what an important and large Roman station it must have been. The Fosse Way, Ermine Street, and Ikenild Street all pass through Corinium, and another Roman road, called the White Way, runs due north.

In a work of this sort it would be out of place to enter upon a detailed description of this celebrated station, teeming with its tesselated pavements, Roman villas, and other objects of interest. They have all been so fully described elsewhere that it seems only necessary to refer the reader to the following authorities :—

    See Buckman's "Corinium."
    Also Atkyn's."History of Gloucestershire."
    Also Rudder's "History of Gloucestershire," p. 343.
    Also "Archæological Journal," vol. vi., p. 321.
    Also "Archæologia," vol. xviii., p. 112.
    Also "Guide to the Museum at Cirencester," by A. H. Church.

No. 34.—CRICKLEY HILL CAMP.

This lies one mile north of the village of Birdlip, in the parish of Cubberley, and four miles south of Cheltenham. It is protected by a mound and ditch running across the projecting height in a slightly curved line, with a second mound and ditch running parallel to the main one, and 100 yards from it. The remaining three sides of the camp are protected by the precipitous nature of the hill. The area defended is about nine acres, and the earthworks still remaining show what an important position it must have been. On the high ground to the east of the camp the defences are much stronger than they are on the lower ground as they approach the escarpment. Unlike most other camps in the county, this has a perfect entrance, defended by an advanced bank and ditch ; and in the immediate neighbourhood are six round barrows and one fine long barrow.

    See "Archæologia," vol. xix., p. 170.
    Also "Proceedings Cott. Nat. Field Club," vol. vi., p. 210.
    Also "Transactions Bristol and Glou. Archæ. Soc.," 1879-80, p. 206.

No. 35.—DAMERY CAMP.

At the south-east corner of Michaelwood Chase, in the parish of Berkeley, there are slight traces of an ancient camp. It was visited by the members of the Cotteswold Field Club in July, 1871. It is situated on the extremity of a hill, near to Damery Bridge, and three miles south-east of Berkeley. Mr. Playne, in describing it, says, "It has an irregular oval shape, about 160 yards long and 40 yards across."

    See "Proceedings Cott. Nat. Field Club.," vol. vi., p. 228.

18   ANCIENT CAMPS.

No. 36.—DOWDESWELL CAMP, No. 1.

This lies in the parish of Dowdeswell, between Rossley Farm and Upper Dowdeswell House, about four miles south-east of Cheltenham. It is quadrilateral in form, and measures 420 yards on one side and 320 yards on the other, while the average width is 220 yards, its area being nearly seventeen acres. The entrenchments on the north and west sides consist of a high mound and ditch; on the south there is a mound only, and on the east the steepness of the escarpment forms a natural defence. The enclosure is divided into two nearly equal portions by a single mound. There is an entrance into the northern portion at the south-west angle, and into the other portion there is an entrance at each of the southern angles. In this latter portion there is an ancient tank, and a good spring of water rises just outside the camp on the eastern side.

See " Transactions Bristol and Glou. Archæ. Soc.," 1879-80, p. 203.

No. 37.—DOWDESWELL CAMP, No. 2.

Half a mile to the east of the earthworks just described are some more extensive entrenchments. They are also in the parish of Dowdeswell, in a field close to Upper Dowdeswell House. The banks on the east and west sides are still very strong, while the north and south sides have nearly disappeared, though a wall is evidently built along the line of the southern bank. Probably both these camps were in some way connected with the extensive Roman station at Wycomb, a little more than a mile distant.

See " Transactions Bristol and Glou. Archæ. Soc.," 1879-80, p. 203.

No. 38.—DOYNTON CAMPS.

These occupied the high rocks on either side of the little river Boyd. One was in the parish of Doynton, the other in the parish of Abston, three miles north-east of Bitton. The stream here runs through a deep ravine, and on each side

ANCIENT CAMPS.

there were fortifications and entrenchments. The remains of earthworks are still to be seen on the west side, but those on the east have entirely disappeared.

See Rudder's "History of Gloucestershire," p. 406.
Also "Proceedings Cott. Nat. Field Club," vol. vi., p. 231.
Also Bigland's "History of Gloucestershire," vol. i., p. 469.

No. 39.—DRAKESTONE.

This ancient signalling station or "outlook" is to be found on the southern point of Stinchcombe Hill, one and a quarter miles west of Dursley, in the parish of Stinchcombe. The point known as Drakestone is defended by a series of banks and ditches, certainly not less than four in number, and yet the area defended is only one-sixteenth part of an acre in extent, far too small for a camp. There is probably no spot in Gloucestershire where grander views can be obtained; it is admirably adapted for a post of observation, at least ten other camps being visible. The remains of 32 pit dwellings have been discovered a little to the north of Drakestone, and it has been suggested that it might have formed a refuge to the pre-historic people who dwelt in these "pits"!

See "Archæologia," vol. xix., p. 166.
Also "Proceedings Cott. Nat. Field Club," vol. vi., p. 216.

No. 40.—DYRHAM CAMP.

This occupies a projecting point of Hinton Hill, in the parish of Dyrham, three miles south of Chipping Sodbury, and seven miles north of Bath. It was defended by a single mound and ditch running on a curved line, with each end resting on the escarpment, thus protecting an area of about 18 acres. On the south side, the slope of the hill has been artificially "scarped," and on the east side a portion of the entrenchment is still very strong. A modern road runs through the camp. Writing in the year 1821, Mr. Baker says, "The ditch is deep and perfect, and the bank high and steep." Camden and Sir

Robert Atkyns state that this camp was used when Ceawlin, King of the West Saxons, obtained his decisive victory over the Britons at the battle of Deorham, in the year 571 or 577.

See Rudder's " History of Gloucestershire," p. 427.
Also " Archæologia," vol. xix., p. 165.
Also " Proceedings Cott. Nat. Field Club," vol. vi., p. 219.

No. 41.—ENGLISH BICKNOR.

There are some interesting earthworks in the parish of English Bicknor, three miles north of Coleford. They have been carefully described by Sir John Maclean, F.S.A., who considers them to date from the 8th or 9th century. They seem to form one of the Castella or Burhs mentioned by Mr. G. T. Clark, in his paper on " Earthworks," in the Archæological Journal, vol. 38, 1881. The works consist of a " conical flat-topped mound or motte, which was originally surrounded by a ditch, but this is now filled up except on the western side, where it is of considerable depth. The motte stands on a horse-shoe shaped platform, also surrounded by a ditch, which is connected with the ditch of the mound." On this platform, and close to the motte, stands the ancient well, supplied by a never-failing spring of water. Beyond this is a second and larger platform (on which stands the parish church), and this is defended by another deep ditch, the whole work forming an irregular circle about 150 yards in diameter. (See description of the earthworks in the parish of Upper Slaughter.) Such was the original character of the work, but at a subsequent period it formed the site of a Norman castle, and further additions were made to the fortifications.

See " Transactions Bristol and Glou. Archæ. Soc.," 1879-80, vol. iv., p. 303.

No. 42.—ELBERTON CAMP.

This occupies a projecting point of a hill in the parish of Elberton, a little to the east of the village, and nine miles north of Bristol. In shape it is an obtuse-angled parallelogram, about 100 yards wide, and the defence consists of two banks with a ditch between them. The view it commands of the neighbouring river Severn is very extensive.

See Atkyn's " History of Gloucestershire," p. 223.
Also Rudder's " History of Gloucestershire," p. 437.
Also " Archæologia," vol xix., p. 163.
Also " Proceedings Cott. Nat. Field Club," vol. vi., p. 230.

No. 43.—Eubury Camp.

This remarkable camp lies in the parish of Condicote, a quarter of a mile east of the village, and two and a half miles north-west of Stow-on-the-Wold. It occupies a projecting spur of the hill, a little to the north-east of the round camp at Condicote, and is surrounded on three sides by shallow valleys. The camp is defended on the south by two steep banks scarped in the side of the hill, and extending for more than 300 yards. On the north side it is defended by a single bank, and it has in addition a remarkable mound running parallel to the main work and 50 yards from it, situated in the lowest part of the narrow valley! This mound is 180 yards in length, 10 feet high, and ends abruptly at each end. The area defended is about eight acres.

See " Proceedings Cott. Nat. Field Club," vol. vi., p. 207.

No. 44.—Frampton Mansell Camp.

This camp, which was destroyed nearly forty years ago, stood on high ground above the village of Frampton Mansell, in the parish of Sapperton, six miles west of Cirencester. The defensive works consisted of two lines running on a curve, enclosing a small area between them and the escarpment. In the year 1759 a large quantity of Roman coins were found close to the camp, at a place called Lark's Bush. Rudder gives a list of these coins.

See Rudder's " History of Gloucestershire," p. 642.
Also " Proceedings Cott. Nat. Field Club," vol. vi., p. 214.

No. 45.—Freezing Hill or Furzen Hill.

There are some earthworks on the southern point of this hill two and a half miles north-east of Bitton. They consist of a bank with a ditch on either side, running nearly parallel to the brow of the hill, and only a short distance from the escarpment. It is difficult to say for what purpose they were intended, but it has been suggested that they formed part of a civil boundary in connection with similar works on Tog Hill.

See " Proceedings Cott. Nat. Field Club," vol. vi., p. 220.

No. 46.—Glevum.

The site of the present city of Gloucester was no doubt a fortified position under the Britons, being their Caer Glou. No signs, however, exist of the British earthworks, but the Roman wall of Glevum has been carefully traced and described by Mr. John Bellows. Beginning opposite Eastgate House, the wall, which is nine feet thick, runs in a S.S.W. direction along Queen Street and Constitution Walk. It next passes into the grounds of Brunswick House, keeping parallel with Brunswick Road as far as the end of Parliament Street. The wall now turns at right angles, and runs in a W.N.W. direction along the back of Parliament Street to the South Gate; it then strikes into Commercial Road, and runs straight to the corner of the County Prison. Here again it turns to the N.N.E., passing the Prison, along the Barbican, close to the Shire Hall, parallel to Berkeley Street, and here it reaches the West Gate. It then runs under the houses of Lower College Court straight for the Cathedral porch. At the Cathedral the Roman wall has been entirely removed to get a good foundation. The north-west angle stood about the centre of the present cloisters, and thence the wall ran straight to the North Gate, opposite Aldate Street, then along the left side of Aldate Street till it reaches King Street, and here is the north-east angle. It then runs straight up this street to Eastgate House, our starting point. A great number of

ANCIENT CAMPS. 23

Roman antiquities have been discovered within this area at various times.

At Kingsholm, a suburb on the north-west side of the city, were some artificial mounds and the traces of a ditch. Some have thought this to be the original site of ancient Gloucester, and some have considered it to be the cemetery of the Roman Glevum.

> See Rudder's "History of Gloucestershire, p. 82.
> Also "Archæologia," vol. x., p. 132.
> Also "Crania Brittanica," vol. ii.
> Also "Gentleman's Magazine," vol. xl. (new series), p. 40.
> Also "Gentleman's Magazine," vol. xliii. (new series), p. 248.
> Also "The Celt, the Roman, and the Saxon," (Wright), p. 161.
> Also "Proceedings Cott. Nat. Field Club," vol. vi., p. 154.
> Also "Transactions Bristol and Glou. Archæ. Soc.," vol. i., p. 153.

No. 47.—Haresfield Camp.

This well-known work crowns the summit of Haresfield Beacon, six miles south of Gloucester. The original British camp, conforming to the irregular shape of the ground, and defended on two sides by the steep escarpment of the hill, extended for nearly 1,000 yards from the "Beacon" at the west end to the "Bulwarks" on Brodbro' Green. These consisted of a bank eighteen feet in height from the bottom of the ditch, the total area enclosed being forty-four acres. The Britons required a considerable space, as their wives, children, and cattle were with them; but the Romans, being a compact body of fighting men, required less room, and cut off about a third of the original area by throwing up a strong bank 30 feet high, 400 yards from the west end, and constructing four gates as usual. There are distinctive marks between the British and Roman work—breastworks are formed at the edge of the escarpments, even where they are the steepest, in the Roman camp, while there is not a trace of anything of the kind in the British. Outside the north gate of the Roman camp is a never-failing well or spring; likewise below the British end of the camp is a similar spring, with a well-marked path leading down to it, but situated at a lower level, and not so carefully protected by embankments as the Roman one. At the west end, the remains of the original Roman road are visible leading into the camp, cutting through two additional entrenchments running across the neck of the hill. In August, 1837, a crock containing nearly 3,000 Roman coins was found inside the south gate. A Roman horse-shoe was also found (described by Fleming). The view from this position is very extensive, including the hills of Malvern, Bredon, Cleeve, Leckhampton, Crickley, Birdlip, Robin's Wood, Churchdown, Selsley, Stinchcombe, &c.; the towns of Gloucester and Tewkesbury; May Hill, the Forest of Dean, the whole range of the Severn, and the Bristol Channel.

See Bigland's " History of Gloucestershire," vol. ii., p. 29.
Also " Archæologia," vol. xix., p. 169.
Also " Proceedings Cott. Nat. Field Club," vol. vi., p. 211.
Also Fosbrooke's " History of Gloucestershire," vol. i., p 303.

No. 48.—HARESFIELD MOAT.

On the north side of Haresfield Church, adjoining the churchyard, is a very striking entrenchment, the work probably of the Saxon or the Dane. It consists of a mound somewhat in the shape of a horse-shoe, standing nearly ten feet above the level of the adjoining land, and measuring 78 yards from north to south and 68 yards from east to west. This mound is surrounded by a deep moat or ditch 18 feet wide and still nine feet deep. In the centre of the mound is a level platform about 35 yards square, standing 2 feet 6 inches high, and between this central platform and the main moat (running parallel to the latter) is a slight ditch and bank, which was probably surmounted by a stockade, the whole work forming a strong vale fort very similar to that at Leckhampton, near Cheltenham. Mr. G. T. Clarke, in his valuable paper on Earthworks in the " Archæological Journal," vol. xxxviii., speaking of moated mounds, says :—" These

ANCIENT CAMPS. 25

works, thrown up in England in the 9th and 10th centuries, are seldom if ever rectangular. First was cast up a truncated cone of earth, standing at its natural slope from 12 to even 50 or 60 feet in height. This 'mound,' 'motte,' or 'burh,' the 'mota' of our records, was formed from the contents of a broad and deep circumscribing ditch." (See description of Leckhampton Moat.)

No. 49.—HAZLEWOOD COPSE CAMP.

There are traces of a considerable defensive work in a copse one mile south-east of Nailsworth, in the parish of Avening. The area enclosed is about ten acres. This is defended by slight mounds and ditches, constructed on curved lines In one part there are three parallel lines, two of which have the ditches outside their mounds, while the third has the ditch inside. Part of the outer line has an elevation of four feet from the bottom of the ditch to the top of the bank, and may have been a later work, added to strengthen the camp, and so constructed that it formed an independent area. Mr. Playne says, "Close to the north side of the camp is a spot, less than an acre in extent, from which I have gathered 2,000 worked flints," and he suggests that this was a dwelling place of the flint folk, having the adjoining camp for a refuge.

See "Proceedings Cott. Nat. Field Club," vol. v., p. 285.
Also "Proceedings Cott. Nat. Field Club," vol. vi., p. 218.

No. 50.—HEBDOWN CAMP.

Two miles north of Marshfield there is marked on the Ordnance Survey "Hebdown Camp." It is situated on the borders of Wiltshire and Gloucestershire; but though the site is well suited for a defensive position, no signs of entrenchments are now to be seen. The projecting point of the hill, on which the camp probably stood, is bounded on three sides by valleys. There is another entrenchment near this. (See Littleton Camp.)

No. 51.—Hempstead Camp.

This lies in the parish of Hempstead, on the brow of the hill, a little to the north of the church, one mile south-west of Gloucester. The defensive works are so indistinct, and in some parts so much obscured by farm buildings, &c., that it is difficult to say anything definite as to the nature of the work; but the late Rev. Samuel Lysons was of opinion that it corresponded with the most perfect form of Roman camp. He says :—" Its form was oblong, 260 yards long by 113 wide, divided into two parts, the upper and lower; the vallum, fossa, and agger must have been of considerable height and depth. There were four gates; one of these led down to the Severn, and the road is still traceable." There seem to have been two ramparts on the north side of the camp, and a raised causeway led from the north-west corner to Gloucester. In 1859, two Roman interments were found to the east of the camp, with some coins, lachrymatories, pottery, and horse bones; and the " Holy Well," or " Our Ladies' Well," is just outside the entrenchments on the west side.

See " The Romans in Gloucestershire," by Lysons, p. 49.
Also " Proceedings Cott. Nat. Field Club," vol. vi., p. 227.

No. 52.—Hewletts Camp.

This is a small work on the top of Hewletts Hill, two miles east of Cheltenham. It is irregular in shape, and is partly defended by having the sides of the hill scarped so as to form a steep slope. On the west side is a ditch and mound defending the weakest point, adjoining the ancient road from Cheltenham to Whittington and Shipton Olive. The greatest length of the protected area is 100 yards, and the greatest breadth 60 yards. It has been suggested that this small work was an outpost connected with the important camps on Nottingham and Cleeve Hills.

See " Transactions Bristol and Glou. Archæ. Soc.," 1879-80, p. 204.

The area defended is about 12 acres, and the earthworks consist of a single mound and ditch running on a curved line, with each end resting on the escarpment. There is an entrance to the camp near the middle of the line, and on the south side of the entrance a second bank has been thrown up on the east side of the ditch.

See "Proceedings Cott. Nat. Field Club," vol. vi., p. 221.

No. 62.—LANSDOWN CAMP, No. 2.

About 300 yards from the last, a square camp is marked on the Ordnance Map. It is in reality 150 yards long and 60 yards wide, and is defended by a very slight mound and ditch. The area thus enclosed is about one acre, and has an entrance on the south side.

See "Proceedings Cott. Nat. Field Club," vol. vi., p. 221.

No. 63.—LANSDOWN CAMP, No. 3.

The Ordnance Map marks an "ancient camp" a quarter of a mile south-west of the Granville Monument, and Mr. Playne considers that it was a fortified position, though it is very unlike any other of our Cotswold camps. "Some seven or eight acres of the hill top are covered with mounds ten to fifteen feet high, with narrow hollows between them." There is no mound or ditch surrounding this network, and I think it would be difficult to find any proof that it was an ancient fort. It is, however, well worth an examination.

See "Proceedings Cott. Nat. Field Club," vol. vi., p 221.

No. 64.—LECKHAMPTON CAMP.

On Leckhampton Hill, two miles south of Cheltenham, there is an interesting work of some magnitude. The point of the hill overlooking the valley of the Severn has been cut off by an entrenchment, consisting, for the greater part of the distance, of a single mound nine feet high, with each end resting on the escarpment. About 50 yards from the northern precipice there are two entrances through the entrenchments, one leading into the main portion of the camp, and another, at a much lower level, leading into a deep depression running nearly parallel with the edge of the rocks. Along the line of the entrenchments from these entrances to the escarpment there is a considerable ditch, outside the bank. On the old Ordnance Survey a bank is shown parallel to the northern escarpment of the hill. This has possibly been destroyed by quarrying operations. Professor Buckman, in his " Corinium," speaks of a true Roman well existing in the centre of the camp, sunk through the various strata of the oolitic rocks down to the clay beneath. I can find no trace of this, but there are one or two likely-looking hollows in which a little excavation might be interesting. On the outside of the camp, towards the east, is a remarkable round barrow, 4 feet high and 35 feet in diameter; this is protected by a mound 70 feet square and 2 feet 6 inches high. At a distance of over 300 yards from the main position is another line of earthworks, consisting of a single bank, in some places five feet high, running on a curved line, and thus enclosing a very large area, probably for flocks and herds. Several relics of antiquity have been found on Leckhampton Hill, including a bronze helmet, spear-heads, coins, pottery, flint arrow-heads, &c.; and some human skeletons have been discovered at various times.

> See " Archæologia," vol. xix., p. 171.
> Also " Archæological Journal," vol. xii., p. 9.
> Also Bigland's " History of Gloucestershire," vol. ii., p. 148.
> Also Buckman's " Corinium," p. 5.
> Also " Proceedings Cott. Nat. Field Club," vol. vi., p. 209.
> Also "Journal of Archæological Association," vol. i., p. 43.
> Also "Transactions Bristol and Glou. Archæ. Soc.," 1879-80, p. 206.

No. 65.—LECKHAMPTON MOAT.

On the north-west side of Leckhampton Church there is a remarkable moated enclosure, which was visited by the members of the Bristol and Gloucestershire Archæological

Society in July, 1879. In shape it is irregular, having five sides of different dimensions. The greatest length from north to south is 80 yards, and greatest breadth from east to west 50 yards. The moat averages 20 feet in width, and is half full of water. On the outside of the moat is a bank, in some places four feet high. This appears to have been continued all round the enclosure. The central mound is nine feet above the water in the moat, and, though on a level with the adjoining land on the west, is ten feet above the original level on the east. In describing this in 1879, I stated that no foundations of any kind had been discovered within the enclosure, and such was the case up to that date; but early in 1881 a considerable number of stones were found by the edge of the moat on the east side, as if forming the foundation of a bridge. They were from four to five feet below the surface, and there are some corresponding foundations visible on the other side of the moat, with remains of a paved road six feet wide, leading from the direction of the church. On the west side of the enclosure a number of worked stones set in mortar were found at the same time, as if forming steps down to the water in the moat. From these discoveries it appears probable that the position was occupied in comparatively recent times, though doubtless it was one of the moated mounds of the 9th or 10th centuries mentioned by Mr. G. T. Clark. There are further earthworks on the north side, which probably formed an outer court connected with the moated enclosure. (See Haresfield Moat.)

No. 66.—LITTLE DEAN CAMP.

In the parish of Little Dean, to the east of the village, and one and a half miles north-west of Newnham, is a camp nearly circular in shape, remarkable for its small size and strong fortifications. A ditch, six feet deep, surrounds a bank twelve feet high, and the area enclosed has a diameter of only seventeen yards in one direction and of 22 yards in the other. There is an entrance on the south-east side. This was probably an outpost of the adjacent camp on Welshbury Hill, and must have been a difficult position to assault, though it would only accommodate a very few men.

See "Proceedings Cott. Nat. Field Club," vol. vi., p. 234.

No. 67.—LITTLETON CAMP.

In the parish of Littleton, two miles north of Marshfield, there are traces of earthworks occupying the projecting point of a hill. This spot is marked on the Ordnance Map as an ancient camp. It is near the boundary of Wiltshire and Gloucestershire, and is defended on three sides by valleys. It is only a quarter of a mile from Hebdown Camp, previously mentioned.

No. 68.—LYDNEY CAMP, No. 1.

On the summit of Camp Hill in Lydney Park, one mile south-west of the town, there are the remains of a fine Roman villa and temple, protected by earthworks running across the promontory and along its eastern side. On the west side there are no earthworks, the escarpment of the hill being very steep. On the north side, where the ridge of the hill is prolonged, there is a deep ditch outside the mound, and at a little distance from this is a second mound. The area thus defended measures about 280 yards by 120 yards, the buildings occupying the south-eastern portion. The situation is admirably selected for defence, the steep slopes of the hill forming a difficult approach on three sides, and water being easily obtained from a fine stream running on the north side. An approach road is still to be traced running up to the camp, and corresponding with the upper end of this is a gateway in the outer wall of the Roman villa. This road has been considerably lowered in comparatively recent times, but part of the original trackway can be seen just before entering the camp. This was doubtless a very important position during the Roman occupation of this country. (See

ANCIENT CAMPS.

Lydney Villa.) The series of coins found extend from Augustus, who died A.D. 14, to Arcadius, who died A.D. 408.

> See " Roman Antiquities at Lydney Park " (Bathurst).
> Also " Archæologia," vol. v., p. 207.
> Also Rudder's "History of Gloucestershire," p. 525.
> Also Fosbrooke's " History of Gloucestershire," vol. ii., p 197.
> Also " Beauties of England and Wales," vol. v., p. 721.

No. 69.—LYDNEY CAMP, No. 2.

This lies close to the last, but is separated from it by a deep valley. It is situated on the termination of a spur of the hill, irregular in shape, and very small in size, the area not being more than half an acre. The defence consists of a single bank and ditch, and there is an inner fort, with additional intrenchments, on the side easiest of access. It appears to be British in type, though it was certainly occupied by the Romans, like so many other of the British camps in Gloucestershire. Some pottery and Roman coins have been found here, also stones, and a capital of a small pillar, belonging probably to a watch tower, for which the position was well adapted, having extensive views of the River Severn and the range of camps on the Cotswold Hills.

> See " Roman Antiquities at Lydney Park " (Bathurst).
> Also " Proceedings Cott. Nat. Field Club," vol. vi., p. 235.
> Also "Archæologia," vol. v., p. 207.

No. 70.—MEON HILL CAMP.

Meon Hill lies at the north of our county, partly in the parish of Lower Quinton, and partly in the parish of Mickleton, six miles south of Stratford-on-Avon. It stands by itself in the vale, and is a conspicuous object for many miles round. The summit of this hill has been fortified. The earthworks forming the defence are irregular in shape, conforming to the contour of the hill. Mr. Playne well describes their nature in the following words :—" There is a very slight mound on the edge of the escarpment; below the edge of the hill the slope has been artificially scarped, giving a very steep bank 18 feet high from the bottom of the ditch; then follows a steep-sided mound eight feet high, and then a third mound five feet high." No less than 394 sword-like blades of iron were discovered in this camp in 1824. They were carefully arranged socket and point, as though they had been packed together in a chest; their average length was 33 inches. One hundred and twenty of the same kind were found in Salmonsbury Camp, near Bourton-on-the-Water, a few years ago.

See Rudder's " History of Gloucestershire," p. 614.
Also "Proceedings Cott. Nat. Field Club," vol. vi., p. 224.

No. 71.—Minchinhampton Camp.

This is on Minchinhampton Common, two and a half miles south of Stroud. It is by far the largest intrenched work in Gloucestershire, its area being nearly 600 acres. The defence consists of a single mound and ditch, running on an irregular curve, the ends of which are more than a mile asunder. It runs nearly due north from a point above the village of Box, and when it reaches the old road to Cirencester it turns to the east, enclosing within its area the present village of Minchinhampton. After passing the village it turns to the south, near "Woeful Danes Bottom," and here it seems to be defended by three parallel lines of earthworks. On the north side the remains of an entrance are still to be seen, there being a passage through the mound and across the ditch. The large area of this work seems to show that it was a settlement of some prehistoric tribe rather than a camp for military purposes.

See Rudder's " History of Gloucestershire," p. 468.
Also " Proceedings Cott. Nat. Field Club," vol. v., p. 285.
Also " Proceedings Cott. Nat. Field Club," vol. vi., p. 214.

ANCIENT CAMPS. 37

No. 72.—NORBURY CAMP, No. 1.

In the parish of Farmington there is a large camp known as Norbury. It lies close to the village, one mile from Northleach, and half a mile to the east of the Fosse Way. It occupies the ridge of a hill, the north and east sides being defended by a single mound. On the south the slope of the hill has been artificially scarped, and on the west a mound and ditch cross the ridge on a curved line. The area thus enclosed is about 80 acres. The intrenchments, though still to be traced, have been much reduced by cultivation in some parts. Towards the west end of the enclosure there is a long barrow, and on the outside stands a round barrow. To the east are the remains of a Roman villa. (See Farmington Villa.) An ancient road, probably the Green Way, seems to run through the camp from east to west; and another old road, called Letch Lane, leads from the east end to Salmonsbury Camp, near Bourton-on-the-Water.

See Atkyn's "History of Gloucestershire," p. 227.
Also Rudder's "History of Gloucestershire," p. 579.
Also "Proceedings Cott. Nat. Field Club," vol. vi., p. 210.
Also "Transactions Bristol and Glou. Archæ. Soc.," 1879-80, p. 206.

No. 73.—NORBURY CAMP, No. 2.

Another camp, locally known as Norbury, lies in the parish of Colesbourn, one mile and a quarter to the north-west of the village. The earthworks defending this position have been very much damaged, but the general form of the camp can still be traced. It is irregular in shape, having an area of about six acres, and is defended by a single mound and ditch. The views from the hill are extensive, and the camp is well selected for defence, and to guard against any attacking party approaching from the south, or south-east, up the narrow valleys which are here to be found threading their way between the Cotswold Hills.

See Rudder's "History of Gloucestershire, p. 383.
Also "Proceedings Cott. Nat. Field Club," vol. vi., p. 210.
Also "Transactions Bristol and Glou. Archæ. Soc.," 1879-80, p. 206.

No. 74.—North Cerney Camp.

In the parish of North Cerney, three and a half miles north of Cirencester, there are some earthworks described by Bigland as "imperfect vestiges of a Roman specula or outpost." From a recent examination of the ground, I find that though there are traces of a small camp, the banks have been so much levelled by cultivation that nothing decisive can be said as to the character of the work. Some few Roman antiquities have been found in this locality, and the ancient White Way, running due north from the Roman town Corinium, is close at hand.

See Bigland's "History of Gloucestershire," vol. i., p. 285.
Also "Beauties of England and Wales," vol. v., p. 667.

No. 75.—Nottingham Hill Camp.

This occupies a projecting promontory of the Cotswold Hills, in the parish of Cleeve, four miles north-east of Cheltenham. It is one of the largest camps in the county, covering an area of 120 acres, formed by a line of earthworks, consisting of two banks and two ditches, running across the neck of the hill. In 1863, during some excavations, the original mound of the Britons and the superstructure of the Romans were laid bare to view. A number of bones, British and Roman coins, lance heads, &c., have been found here at different times. Rudder mentions several of round barrows, both inside and outside the camp; but they have all disappeared.

See "Archæologia," vol. xix., p. 171.
Also Rudder's "History of Gloucestershire," p. 369.
Also Norman's "History of Cheltenham," p. 12.
Also "Proceedings Cott. Nat. Field Club," vol. vi., p. 209.
Also "Transactions Bristol and Glou. Archæ. Soc.," 1879-80, p. 206.

No. 76.—Offa's Dyke.

This celebrated civil boundary was erected in the year 779 A.D., by King Offa, as a boundary between the Welsh and the Saxons; and in the Laws of Ina, another Saxon king, we read that any Welshman caught with weapons on him on the English side of the Dyke was to lose his right hand. The Dyke, which consists of a mound from 8 to 15 feet high and 40 feet wide, with a ditch on each side, runs from the Severn Sea to the mouth of the Dee. It has been carefully traced by Sir John Maclean through this county. Beginning in Sedbury Park, on the bank of the Severn, it can be traced running across the Beachley promontory to the banks of the Wye ; then, following the edge of the cliffs which tower above that river, it runs by Denhel Hill Wood, above the "Devil's Pulpit," overlooking Tintern Abbey, by Caswell Wood, across St. Briavel's Common, through St. Margaret's Grove, Redhill Grove, &c; it can then be traced from Bicknor to Lydbrook, where it extends round the outer bend of the river and leaves the county. It then continues through parts of Herefordshire, Radnorshire, Flintshire, and Denbighshire. In length it is about one hundred miles, and was no doubt a civic boundary ; but there are points in it of such strength that it seems probable they were intended for military positions.

See "Proceedings Cott. Nat. Field Club," vol. vi., p. 257.
Also "Transactions Bristol and Glou. Archæ. Soc.," 1880-81.

No. 77 AND 78.—OLDBURY CAMPS.

In the parish of Oldbury-on-Severn, two miles north-west of Thornbury, are two ancient camps near the River Severn— one on the south side of Oldbury Pill, the other on the north side, guarding the harbour. The one on the south side is small, on a conical hill, at the top of which stands the church. Round the churchyard traces of the banks can still be traced. The one on the north side is on a slight elevation, and is formed by a mound and ditch. This is locally known as "The Toots." It is a large camp, the area enclosed being about 10 acres. At the south angle the ditch is broad, and nearly twelve feet deep. Many Roman coins have been found here.

See Atkyn's " History of Gloucestershire."
Also Rudder's " History of Gloucestershire."
Also " Proceedings Cott. Nat. Field Club," vol. vi., p. 229.
Also " Archæologia," vol. xix., p. 163.

No. 79.—Oldbury Court Camp.

On the hill above Oldbury Court, in the parish of Stapleton, four miles north-east of Bristol, Rudder says there was a small camp which gave the name to the house. I have not been able to visit this locality, but the owner of the property informs me that he is unable now to trace any defensive works.

See Rudder's " History of Gloucestershire," p. 693.

No. 80.—Oxenton Hill Camp.

On Oxenton Hill, six miles north of Cheltenham, in the parish of Oxenton, there are remains of an ancient camp. It is irregular in form, the line of defence following the contour of the hill. On the north and east sides the steepness of the escarpment, with some artificial assistance, forms a sufficient defence. On the south and west sides, in addition to the scarping of the steep slope, a strong bank has been constructed about twenty feet from the foot of the "scarp," thus forming a considerable work. Inside the camp the ground is very irregular, and there is certainly one round barrow still in existence; probably there are more, but without excavation it is impossible to say. The views from the top of Oxenton Hill are very extensive, and in every way the position seems well adapted for a British stronghold.

No. 81.—Pinbury Camp.

In the hamlet of Pinbury, four and a half miles north-west of Cirencester, are the remains of an ancient work. A projecting part of the hill in Pinbury Park had a single mound running across it, and the extreme point of the camp was also defended, the enclosed area being about one acre.

A house was built here during the last century, the area of the camp formed into a bowling green, and the principal mound into a terrace walk.

See Rudder's " History of Gloucestershire," p. 424.
Also "Proceedings Cott. Nat. Field Club," vol. vi., p. 212.

No. 82.—PRESTBURY EARTHWORKS.

There are some curious earthworks in the parish of Prestbury, a quarter of a mile west of the church, and two miles from Cheltenham. They are divided into two parts, each of them rectangular in shape. The strongest portion, and that best preserved, measures 155 yards by 130 yards, the defence consisting of a bank and deep ditch. Unlike the camps on the Cotswold Hills, the ditch is inside the bank. In the centre of the enclosure are some traces of stone foundations. For what purpose these intrenchments were intended, or to what age they belong, we are unable to say, though various suggestions have been made.

See "Trans. Bristol and Glou. Archæ. Soc.," 1879-80, p. 204.
Also "Notes on Cheltenham, Ancient and Mediæval," by W. H. Gomonde, 1849.

No. 83.—PUCKHAM CAMP.

There is an intrenchment in Puckham Scrubs, in the parish of Sevenhampton, four miles east of Cheltenham, the nature of which is so peculiar that no one has been able to give a satisfactory explanation as to its origin. A deep ditch runs on a curved line for nearly 200 yards, and on the outside of the ditch is a bank five feet high, the ditch in some places being twelve feet deep. This intrenchment terminates abruptly at each end, apparently from the fact that it was unfinished. The position is admirably suited for a hill fort, and the defence, so far as it goes, has been constructed with great care. In the " Anthropological Review," vol. iii., p. 70, mention is made of a large round barrow on this hill, but I have been unable to find any trace of it. Adjoining this intrenchment are several hundred pit-like depressions, which are worthy of close examination.

No. 84.—RANBURY CAMP.

This is situated four miles east of Cirencester, in the parish of Ampney or Eastington. It is irregular in shape, the area defended being about twenty acres. In some places the bank is twelve feet above the bottom of the ditch, in other places the traces of the intrenchment are very slight, though the original shape of the camp can be seen. It stands on high ground about two miles south of the Ikenild Street, and the same distance north-west of the Ermine Street.

See " Proceedings Cott. Nat. Field Club," vol. vi., p. 216.

No. 85.—RANDWICK CAMP.

This is on the top of Randwick Hill, two miles north-west of Stroud. The earthworks consist of a single mound and ditch running across the neck of the hill, with each end resting on the escarpment. The length of this line is about 220 yards, and in some places the bank is still five feet above the bottom of the ditch. Within the defended area there are three barrows, one long and two round. There may have been an outpost on Doverow Hill, three-quarters of a mile south-west of this position, where the natural slope of the hill has been scarped in two parallel lines. The views from Randwick Hill are very grand, embracing the whole vale of the Severn and the entrance to the Stroud valley.

No. 86.—RODBOROUGH CAMP.

On Rodborough Hill, one mile south of Stroud, there are remains of a strong earthwork, now nearly destroyed. A single mound and ditch, running for a short distance, alone remain to mark the site of what was probably a strong encampment. Mr. Playne says there are upwards of 400 ancient pit-dwellings on this hill.

See " Proceedings Cott. Nat. Field Club.," vol. vi., p. 286.
Also Rudder's " History of Gloucestershire," p. 629.

No. 87.—Saintbury Camp.

This lies in the parish of Saintbury, just above the church, two miles north-west of Broadway. Locally it is known as Castle Bank. It is defended on the north side by two ditches and a bank, and there are also earthworks defending a portion of the west side. There are no intrenchments on the south. This is explained by the fact that it was probably an outlying work connected with the much larger camp of Willersey, situated on the hill top, only half a mile distant. There is a round barrow within the defended area. It is interesting to notice that in the Doomsday Book Saintbury is called Suineberie, which is said to mean Swains Camp.

See Rudder's " History of Gloucestershire," p. 635.
Also " Proceedings Cott. Nat. Field Club," vol. vi., p. 207.

No. 88.—Salmonsbury.

This remarkable camp is to be found in the parish of Bourton-on-the-Water, a quarter of a mile north-east of the village. It is nearly rectangular in shape, the defended area being about 60 acres. The earthworks consisted of a single mound of great strength, with a deep and wide ditch on the outside. In some parts these works have been much levelled, but a portion of the north-east side is well preserved, and all the intrenchments can be traced. The situation of this camp, occupying as it does low-lying land in the valley, has puzzled many an antiquary. Rudder says the camp was Roman, and no doubt many valuable Roman antiquities have been found here; but judging from its position, its size, and the character of the masonry forming a wall now covered by the mound, it appears to be the work of pre-Roman times. The wall just mentioned was opened for the inspection of the members of the Cotteswold Field Club in June, 1881. It was about five feet in height, built with thin stones without mortar, and in appearance very much resembled the walling found in barrows. The southern defence extends for more than 200 yards in an easterly direction beyond the rectangular area, and then turns at right angles towards the north, but after turning it can only be traced for a very short distance. There is some very good walling visible in this projection of the defences.

The ancient Fosse Way runs within half a mile of Salmonsbury, and Rudder mentions a paved aqueduct running round a portion of the camp. In a charter dated 779 the following passage occurs :—" Est k portio ruriculi illius attinens urbi illi qui nominabatur Sulmonnes burg."

To give a list of the various objects of interest found in this camp would occupy too much space, but mention must be made of a Roman signet ring of gold weighing nearly an ounce, a great number of Roman coins, and 120 remarkable sword-like blades of iron. These were about 34 inches long, with the metal at one end bent into imperfectly formed sockets. When found they were all carefully arranged socket and point, as though they had been packed together in a chest. Similar weapons have been found at Hod Hill, near Blandford, in Dorset, and no less than 394 within the camp at Meon Hill, in this county. Antiquaries differ very much in opinion as to the date of these, but Mr. Roach Smith, in his " Collectanea Antiqua," vol. v., p. 1, suggests that they were " imperfect swords, fabricated from native iron, and prepared for the final strokes of the war smith ; " and Mr. T. Wright is of opinion that they belong to a late period of the Roman occupation.

See Atkyn's " History of Gloucestershire," p. 153.
Also Rudder's " History of Gloucestershire," p. 303.
Also " Proceedings Cott. Nat. Field Club," vol. vi., p. 209.
Also " Antiquarian Discourses," 1, pref. xix.

No. 89.—Salperton Camp.

This lies high up on the Cotswold Hills, outside Salperton Park, three-quarters of a mile south-west of the village, and four miles north-west of Northleach. The camp was rectangular in form, measuring 80 yards by 60 yards, the defended area being close upon one acre. The intrenchments consisted of a single mound and ditch, now nearly obliterated, with the exccption of the four angles and the whole of the north side. The old Salt Way runs close by this camp, and there are several barrows in the immediate vicinity, both round and long.

See " Transactions Bristol and Glou. Archæ. Soc.," 1879-80, p. 204.

No. 90.—SELSLEY HILL CAMP.

On Selsley Hill, in the parish of King Stanley, two and a half miles south-west of Stroud, there are slight traces of a British camp. An area of about 30 acres is defended by a mound and ditch running on an irregular line. Mr. Playne says there is another very slight earthwork near the neck of the hill, where on one side lies Pen Wood, and on the other Bos-Pen, names which tell of a British occupation. Upwards of 130 pit dwellings have been noticed within the encampment, but not one has been found on the hill outside the lines of defence.

See " Proceedings Cott. Nat. Field Club," vol. v., p. 286.
Also " Proceedings Cott. Nat. Field Club," vol. vi., p. 213.

No. 91.—SHERSTON CAMP.

This is in the parish of Great Sherston, in Wiltshire, four miles south of Tetbury, and only a short distance from the boundary of our county. Most of the village of Sherston is built within a strong fortified earthwork on a point of land between two streams, the most perfect part of which is to the west of the church. Mr. J. Jones, in an interesting contribution to the Proceedings of the Cotteswold Field Club referred to below, suggests that this was the ancient city of " White Walls." At a short distance north-east of Sherston is another intrenched camp, said to have been constructed by the Saxons, but probably older. The Fosse Way runs within one and a half miles of Great Sherston.

See " Proceedings Cott. Nat. Field Club," vol. vi., p. 191.
Also " Murray's Handbook to Wiltshire," p. 20.

No. 92.—SODBURY CAMP.

This well known Roman camp is situated in the parish of Chipping Sodbury, two miles east of the town, and eleven miles due north of Bath. The defended area, which contains upwards of twelve acres, is rectangular in shape, with the west side resting on the escarpment of the hill, the other three sides being defended by a double line of intrenchments, each consisting of a single bank and ditch. There are entrances both on the east and west sides, the camp in all respects being very perfect in form. Mr. King says :—"This seems to have been incomparably well adapted to have contained three cohorts, with double the number of allied foot and half as many more allied horse, encamped after the Polybrian method." King Edward IV. is supposed to have camped here before his celebrated march along the brow of the Cotteswold Hills, from Sodbury to Cheltenham and Tewkesbury, before the "Battle of Tewkesbury."

See " Archæologia," vol. xix., p. 165.
Also Atkyn's "History of Gloucestershire," p. 354.
Also King's "Munimenta Antiqua," vol. ii., p. 148.
Also Rudder's "History of Gloucestershire," p. 676.
Also Lyson's "Woodchester."
Also Fosbrooke's "History of Gloucestershire," vol. ii., p. 29.
Also " Proceedings Cott. Nat. Field Club," vol. iii., p. 54.
Also " Proceedings Cott. Nat. Field Club," vol. vi., p. 219.

No. 93.—SOWDLEY CAMP.

This is at Sowdley Green, in the Forest of Dean, two miles west of Newnham. The enclosed area is very small, not more than one-eighth of an acre in extent. It is situated at the end of a ridge called "Scilly Point." The defences on the north and west are very strong, consisting of a mound of great strength, with a ditch outside; on the south side the escarpment of the hill forms a natural defence, and on the east there is only a slight mound.

See " Proceedings Cott. Nat. Field Club," vol. vi., p. 235.

Nos. 94 and 95.—Stokeleigh Camps.

These camps are in the Stokeleigh Woods, on the Somersetshire side of the Avon, exactly opposite the Clifton Camp. The larger of the two, sometimes known as Rownham Hill Camp, must have been a fine work, with an area of seven acres. On the east it is bounded by the precipice of the river Avon; the remaining sides are defended by three ramparts and two ditches running on a curved line, with each end resting on the escarpment. The second and smaller camp also crowns the precipice of the Avon, a valley separating it from the larger one. The ramparts of this are composed of dry walling, without any lime.

See "History and Antiquities of the City of Bristol," by W. Barrett.
Also "Archæologia," vol. xliv., p. 430.

No. 96.—Stow Green Camp.

Three miles south of Coleford, in the parish of St. Briavels, there is a very small camp, circular in form, known as "Castle Tump." It stands on Bearse Common, and is defended by a strong and high mound. The ditch outside the bank is slight. The defended area is only 35 yards in diameter.

See "Proceedings Cott. Nat. Field Club," vol. vi., p. 235.

No. 97.—Symonds' Yat Intrenchment.

This lies in the parish of English Bicknor, three miles north of Coleford. It occupies a fine promontory of the river Wye. The defence consists of five banks and five ditches running on a curved line across the peninsular, with each end resting on the precipice. The inner bank is 14 feet above the bottom of the corresponding ditch. The banks are about 60 feet apart. Mr. Playne states the defended area to be 650 acres. This work has been often described as of Roman origin, but Sir John Maclean, who has given an excellent description of it in the Proceedings of our County Archæological Society, considers it to belong to the Saxon period, and there seems every reason to believe that he is correct, as no coins or other Roman antiquities have ever been found within the lines of the intrenchment.

    See " Proceedings Cott. Nat. Field Club," vol. vi., p. 233.
    Also " Transactions Bristol and Glou. Archæ. Soc.," 1879-80, p. 301.

No. 98.—Tetbury Camp.

Though the earthworks of the ancient camp at Tetbury have disappeared, it may be useful to record the fact that intrenchments were in existence on the south-east side of the town in the last century. The site of this camp is now a grass field; the form of the terraced walks and slopes remain, but the banks and ditches have gone. Rudder, writing in the year 1779, says:—"The camp was levelled a few years ago by the owner of the land, when several arrow heads, javelins, ancient horse shoes, Roman and Early English coins, &c., were found." Fosbrooke says that this was a British camp, and that it was called Caer-bladon.

    See Rudder's " History of Gloucestershire," p. 727.
    Also Fosbrooke's " History of Gloucestershire," vol. i., p. 401.
    Also " Proceedings Cott. Nat. Field Club," vol. vi., p. 219.

No. 99.—Toddington Camp.

In Toddington Deer Park, two miles north of Winchcombe, there are traces of an intrenched position. The slope of the highest point of the hill has been artificially scarped so as to form a very steep bank about ten feet in height. This bank can be traced round the west, north, and east sides of the hill, enclosing an area of nearly ten acres. No defence is visible on the south side. There is an entrance on the west of the camp, and an old road leads from it into the valley. The views from this point, now turned into a rabbit warren, are very extensive.

ANCIENT CAMPS. 49

No. 100.—Tog Hill Camp.

On the top of Tog Hill, which lies three miles to the west of Marshfield, and four miles from Bath, there are traces of ancient intrenchments, but so slight that very little can be said about them. Mr. Playne, in describing them, says:—"A mound has been thrown up nearly parallel to the brow of the hill. It has a deep ditch on the side towards the escarpment, and a shallow ditch on the other side." There is another slight ditch more to the east.

See "Proceedings Cott. Nat. Field Club," vol. vi., p. 220.

No. 101.—Towbury Camp.

This is in the parish of Twining, about three miles north of Tewkesbury. It is nearly rectangular in shape, the defended area containing more than 20 acres. The defences, which run nearly round the level top of a low hill, consist of a slight bank and deep ditch; but at the south-east angle there is a double mound. It has been supposed by Leland to be a palace of King Offa, but there seems very little evidence of this. It may very likely be of Roman origin, but I think it is one of those works more safely described simply as an "ancient camp."

See Rudder's "History of Gloucestershire," p. 780.
Also "Proceedings Cott. Nat. Field Club," vol. vi., p. 219.

No. 102.—Trajectus.

This Roman station, mentioned in the "Itinerary" of Antonine, has, like Abone, been the subject of much controversy, but I shall again take Bishop Clifford's solution of the difficulty as the most probable one. He places the site of Trajectus at Bitton, five miles north-west of Bath, and points out that a road running from the Stone Circles of Stanton Drew to those in Tracey Park would cross the Avon at Bitton, and probably a settlement would grow up near the passage, which would be translated by the Romans "Trajectus." A

Roman camp, square in form, several Roman villas, and other remains, show that Bitton was a place of great importance during the Roman occupation.

See " Transactions Bristol and Glou. Archæ. Soc.," 1878-79, p. 88.

No. 103.—TREWSBURY CAMP.

This in the parish of Coates, three miles south-west of Cirencester. A large house has been erected within the intrenchments, and in laying out the gardens and grounds much damage has been done to the old earthworkss. They stand on a slightly elevated mound, near the celebrated spring of water known as the Thames Head. There were two banks and ditches on the south and east sides, the west side being naturally defended by the steep escarpment. The area enclosed is about seventeen acres. It was probably a Roman camp, situated close to that part of the Fosse Way called the Acman Street ; but why one so large was required within such a short distance of Corinium it is difficult to say.

See Rudder's " History of Gloucestershire," p. 392.
Also " Proceedings Cott. Nat. Field Club," vol. iii., p. 124.
Also " Proceedings Cott. Nat. Field Club," vol. vi., p. 215.

No. 104.—ULEY BURY.

This well-known camp crowns the top of a lofty hill in the parish of Uley, six miles south-west of Stroud. The peninsular on which it is placed is connected with the adjoining elevation, known as Crawley Hill, by a very narrow neck of land. The fortifications consist of a narrow terrace about seven feet wide, placed at a variable distance, but generally 60 feet down the steep slope of the hill, and of a low rampart made of loose stones covered with turf, on the verge of the descent. This has a broad level space, 45 feet wide, behind it. The shape of the hill-top is nearly quadrangular. There are two entrances, one at the south-east angle and one at the northern angle. The northern or principal entrance is defended by a lofty mound raised upon the ramparts, and three ditches, with their corresponding banks, running across the narrow ridge, which is only 50 yards wide, the sides of which descend very precipitously. The dimensions of the camp are nearly as follows :—S.E. side, 700 paces ; N.E. side, 320 paces ; N.W. side, 800 paces ; S.W. side, 300 paces. A large number of flint arrow heads and Roman coins have been found within the intrenchment. It is rightly looked upon as one of the most remarkable camps in the county.

See "Archæological Journal," vol. xi., p. 328.
Also "Archæologia," vol. xix., p. 167.
Also Atkyn's "History of Gloucestershire," p. 416.
Also Rudder's "History of Gloucestershire," p. 782.
Also "Proceedings Cott. Nat. Field Club," vol. vi., p. 213.

No. 105.—UPPER SLAUGHTER "BURH."

In the parish of Upper Slaughter, three miles south-west of Stow-on-the-Wold, there is a remarkable intrenched work, which has long been a puzzle to local antiquaries. On high ground in the centre of the village stands a mound 80 feet in diameter, with a table-top nearly flat. This is surrounded by a steep slope, about fifteen feet in depth ; then comes an irregular court about 80 feet wide, then another steep slope, at the bottom of which runs a tributary of the river Windrush, along the northern side of the work, while on the eastern side is a moat nearly six feet deep, now used as a road. Outside this court, and further to the east, is an outer court, defended on the north and east sides by the stream, and on the west side by a single mound still about four feet in height, running from the edge of the stream to the moat. On the table-top of the mound there were three slight depressions, and in making an excavation in one of these in 1877 I found that the mound for a depth of seven feet was artificial ; I then came to the original level of the ground, and in continuing the excavation found a circular well, carefully walled with stones. In clearing out this well, which was filled with loose stones, we found a great quantity of charcoal, burnt stones, coarse pottery, bone pins, and various bones of animals. Such is a brief description of the work, similar in some respects to the one at English Bicknor, and forming probably one of the post-Roman Castella or Burhs described by Mr. G. T. Clarke, in his paper on "Earthworks," in the Archæological Journal, vol. xxxviii., 1881.

No. 106.—Welshbury Camp.

This crowns the summit of Welshbury Hill, in the parish of Flaxley, three miles north of Newnham. The area defended measures about 500 feet by 300 feet, and is defended on one side by three ramparts. This was probably a very important camp of the Silures, being the nearest camp to the Roman boundary. The prospect from the summit of the hill is very extensive, and commands a view of a great number of the Cotswold camps on the opposite side of the valley.

See "A Week's Holiday in the Forest of Dean," p. 72.
Also " Proceedings Cott. Nat. Field Club," vol. vii., p. 10.

No. 107.—Willersey Camp.

This is to be found on the summit of the hills in the parish of Willersey, one and a half miles north-east of Broadway. It is a large camp, containing about 60 acres, and there is no doubt the smaller camp of Saintbury, a little to the north, was an outpost of this. The defence consists of two mounds, with a ditch between them, on the west side; on the south and east sides, of a single mound and ditch, in some places very strong; on the north side the escarpment of the hill forms a natural defence. There is an entrance towards the north, and an ancient trackway is seen leading down the hill to the village of Willersey. The remains of a long barrow still exist within the camp, though much levelled by cultivation.

See Rudder's "History of Gloucestershire," pp. 635 and 823.
Also "Proceedings Cott. Nat. Field Club," vol. vi., p. 207.

ANCIENT CAMPS. 53

No. 108.—WINDRUSH CAMP.

This lies one mile south-west of the village of Windrush, and four miles east of Northleach. It is circular in form, and is defended by a single mound about five feet high, with a ditch on the outside about two feet deep, the area thus defended being three acres. An entrance can be traced on the south side. It occupies the highest part of the table land in the vicinity, and has extensive views, including the White-horse hills.

See Rudder's " History of Gloucestershire," p. 830.
Also " Proceedings Cott. Nat. Field Club," vol. vi., p. 210.

No. 109.—WOLSTON CAMP.

I have seen a description of a camp on Wolston Hill, about five miles north of Cheltenham, but having carefully examined the ground I am unable to find any satisfactory traces of such a camp. Should there have been any fortified position here it would probably be only an outpost of the more important work on the summit of Oxenton Hill.

See " Transactions Bristol and Glou. Archæ. Soc.," 1879-80, p. 207.

No. 110.—WOODBURY CAMP.

This is in the parish of Castle Combe, in Wiltshire, about eight miles north-east of Bath, and near the Fosse Way. It is so near the boundary of our county, and in such an interesting parish, that it seems almost necessary to call attention to it in this work. The camp occupies the summit of a steep hill, its area being nearly eight acres. The defence consisted of a single mound and deep ditch. There are other trenches cutting across the area thus enclosed, dividing it into four unequal compartments, one within another. A Norman castle was built within this camp. A fine long barrow known as Lugbury, an interesting Roman villa, and other objects of interest to the antiquary, have been discovered near Castle Combe.

See " History of Castle Combe," by G. Poulet Scrope.

No. 111.—Yewbury Camp.

The earthworks described by Mr. Playne under the head of "Yewbury Camp" occupy the high ground on Woodcroft Common, in the parish of Tidenham, one and a half miles north-east of Chepstow. The traces of earthworks are so very slight that it was with some difficulty I found them, and I think it extremely doubtful if it ever was occupied as an intrenched position.

See "Proceedings Cott. Nat. Field Club," vol. vi., p. 236.

No. 112.—Huddinknoll Hill Intrenchments.

There are some remains of ancient earthworks on Huddinknoll Hill, in the parish of Painswick, on the brow of the Cotswolds, between Kimsbury and Haresfield camps. In the immediate vicinity are a number of pit-like depressions, which may have been ancient habitations, and one of the oldest inhabitants can remember when the intrenchment formed a distinct camp, though now it is difficult to trace the form of it. An ancient trackway, called the "Old Hill Road," runs down the hill towards the village of Brookthorpe, and this was undoubtedly defended by a series of earthworks on the hill top. The field to the south of this road is called "Buckholt," and in this further intrenchments can be traced. In "Bibliotheca Gloucestrensis" an account is given of a sharp encounter at this spot during the Civil Wars and the siege of Gloucester; but there seems strong evidence that the works are of far more ancient construction.

END OF CAMPS.

ROMAN VILLAS.

No. 1.—Bibury Villa.

In the year 1880 a Roman villa was accidentally discovered in the parish of Bibury, about six miles north-east of Cirencester. Some Roman pottery, coins, remnants of tesselated pavements, &c., were found, but as no examination has yet taken place, no description of the building can be given.

No. 2.—Bisley Villa.

This is in a field called the Church Piece, near "Lillyhorn," in the parish of Bisley, about four miles east of Stroud. It was discovered by Mr. T. Baker in 1845, and consists of 29 rooms, occupying a space of 318 feet by 274 feet. Some of the rooms had tesselated pavements. The bricks used in the building were from 7 to 10 inches square and 1 inch thick, the greater part of them being marked in Roman capitals T P F A. In this villa were found fragments of red and coloured pottery, ornamented with a variety of figures; portions of glass ; many implements of brass, such as tweezers ; two knives, part of an adze, and a quantity of bones ; also a round earthern pot, containing a globular mass of metal. This mass was found to consist of 1,223 Roman coins. Some of them were preserved in the state of cohesion in which they were found, and the whole form nearly a complete series, in the best preservation, from the reign of Valerian, who obtained possession of the Empire A.D. 254, to Diocletian, who abdicated A.D. 305. No less than 629 of the coins belonged to Tetricus. They are now in the possession of Mr. Charles Driver, of Lillyhorn.

See "Journal Archæ. Assoc.," vol. i., p. 44.
Also "Archæological Journal," vol. ii., p. 42.
Also "Journal Archæ. Assoc.," vol. ii., p. 324.
Also "Transactions Bristol and Glou. Archæ. Soc.," 1880-81, p. 14.

No. 3.—BOURTON VILLA.

This is situated close to the river Windrush, in the parish of Bourton-on-the-Water, and half a mile west of the village. The Fosse Way runs close by the site of the villa. Great numbers of roofing slates, similar in shape and material to those found at Chedworth, have been found at different times. Foundations, which were from five to six feet high, have been discovered, though no systematic excavation has yet been carried out. The relics found here are such as would only be found in the higher class of Roman villas—rings, in bronze and gilt; pins, in ivory, bronze, and gilt; small fragments of highly ornamented glass, with large quantities of pottery. Portions of upwards of fifty Samian vessels were discovered by Mr. J. Moore. The Roman coins were principally of the Constantine period, but there was a continuous chain of coinage, extending from the time of Aurelius Verus to that of Constans, so that the probability is that the building was inhabited for a period of 200 years. In excavating a portion of this villa in June, 1881, on the occasion of a visit of the Cotteswold Field Club, I discovered upwards of 100 coins, principally of Valens, Valentinian, Constantine, Gratian, &c., but some belonging to Licinius, Probus, Crispus, Tetricus, and Salonina; also a large quantity of pottery, some glass, a "discus," a small iron lamp of curious construction, nails, locks, &c., and the base of a column, 9 inches in diameter and 18 inches high.

No. 4.—BROWN'S HILL VILLA.

In the grounds of the house at Brown's Hill, one mile north of Stroud, were found several portions of Roman tesselated pavement, Roman tiles, coins, pottery, &c. These were discovered in the year 1797, and give certain evidence of the existence of a Roman villa.

See "Roman Antiquities at Woodchester," by S. Lysons, p. 19.

No. 5.—CHEDWORTH VILLA.

This celebrated Roman villa is situated in the parish of Chedworth, about sixteen miles from Gloucester, seven from Cirencester, and three miles west of Fosse Bridge. It was discovered in 1866 by Mr. J. Farrer, and the excavations were carried out by the Earl of Eldon, on whose property the villa stands. He has also erected a museum for the safe custody of all objects of interest found, and buildings to protect the tesselated pavements, which are left in situ. The villa occupies three sides of a square ; the principal buildings face nearly due east, and include an elaborate and complete Roman bath. There were upwards of forty rooms and passages, and these were approached from corridors running the entire length of the villa. Several of the rooms still retain their tesselated pavements. The principal one is 29 feet long by 19 feet wide, and this space, judging from the arrangement of the pavements, was in all probability divided into two parts by a screen or curtain. The pavements display a high degree of artistic skill, especially in the borders. The larger room has a pictorial illustration representing a dance, which appears to be emblematical of the Seasons, from the figures in the corners ; one of which, indicative of winter, has a man warmly clothed, holding a hare or rabbit in his hand. The Roman bath is one of the most perfect to be found in England, having its sweating and cooling chambers, rooms for hot and cold baths, &c. The stone steps in the doorway leading out of the hot room has been much worn by the feet of the Romans some 1400 years ago.

Some large masses of pig iron were found in a compartment which is supposed to have been a blacksmith's shop. One other compartment calls for attention, containing as it does a very perfect collection of pilæ, all of which are standing exactly as found. To allude to the various objects found, such as pottery, implements of iron, bronze, silver, lead, bones, horseshoes, glass, shellfish, &c., would occupy too much space ; but I would particularly draw attention to a very perfect pair of compasses in the museum, 6½ inches long, the legs and rivet of which are most elaborately ornamented. Our mathematical instruments of the present day show little or no improvement on this.

See "Notes on the Roman Villa at Chedworth," 1873.
Also "Proceedings Cott. Nat. Field Club," vol. iv., p. 201.
Also "Proceedings Cott. Nat. Field Club," vol. iv., p. 233.

No. 6.—CHERINGTON VILLA.

This is in a field called Hailston, in the parish of Cherington, three miles from Rodmarton, and seven miles south-west of Cirencester. In 1795 Mr. Lysons found a Roman building here, consisting of seven divisions, covering a space of 82 feet by 54 feet. The walls were two feet high. A great number of Roman coins were found, but no tesselated pavements or flues. It is therefore probable, Mr. Lysons says, that the building was used either for the purposes of agriculture or manufacture.

See "Archæologia," vol. xviii., p. 117.

No. 7.—COMBEND VILLA.

In 1779, some labourers digging for stone in a field called "Stockwoods," at Combend, in the parish of Colesbourne, six miles north-west of Cirencester, discovered the remains of a considerable Roman villa. The floor of one room, 56 feet by 14 feet, was preserved entire, the walls remaining in many places three feet high. Above the pavement were found many of the slates with which the roof had been covered. On the south side of the above was a small coppice. This was grubbed up in 1787 for the purpose of digging stone for building, which seemed to lie very near the surface. The men employed soon found that this appearance arose from the ruins of a very large building, and, finding stone ready to their hand, they immediately pulled down all that remained of the walls, and piled up the material in heaps to the amount of at least 200 cart-loads. It appears there were six rooms parallel to each other, about twelve feet square. On the west side were two rooms of much larger dimensions, and at the opposite end was a hypocaust, evident from the large quantity of square bricks, fragments of flues, &c. Near these were found two columns broken in the middle, still to be seen in the cottage garden. The walls were four feet high, and stuccoed on the inside. Two of the rooms had tesselated pavements, on one of which were many figures of birds and fishes. In the corner of one room was a human skeleton. Many fragments of glass were found among the ruins, which had evidently been used in the windows. It is probable that glass was used by the Romans at a very early period for this purpose, large quantities having been found at Pompeii. Other buildings were found by Mr. Lysons in 1794, consisting of a room 38 feet by 15 feet, pottery, iron hatchets, several Roman coins of Valentinian, Valens, and Gratian. Another room was 20 feet long and 13 feet wide, with tesselated pavement in one corner. There were two other rooms, one with a tesselated pavement nearly entire, ornamented with circles and a double fret border, and the passage, which was five feet wide, had a mosaic pavement with a chequered centre of blue and white, bordered with stripes of brown.

See "Archæologia," vol. ix., p. 319.
Also "Archæologia," vol. xviii., p. 112.
Also King's "Munimenta Antiqua," vol. ii., p. 179.
Also Bigland's "History of Gloucestershire," vol. i., p. 409.

No. 8.—CROMHALL VILLA.

This lies in the parish of Cromhall, two miles from Tortworth Court. It was examined by the Earl of Ducie in 1855. The foundations of several rooms and passages were discovered, a tesselated pavement 18 feet long and 15 feet wide, also a hypocaust. Several Roman coins, portions of pottery, &c., were also found.

See "Archæological Journal," vol. xvii., p. 332.
Also Rudder's "History of Gloucestershire," p. 397.

No. 9.—CORINIUM.

The villas of this well known Roman town have been so fully described by others, that it seems out of place to enter into details here. In that valuable work, " Remains of Roman Art in Cirencester, the Site of Corinium," by Buckman and Newmarch, a description will be found of the architecture, tesselated pavements, hypocausts, and frescoes; also an accurate description of the villa in Dyer Street, and the various kinds of pottery, coins, implements, and ornaments discovered at different times. Then, in the "Guide to the Corinium Museum," by A. H. Church, an interesting account will be found of the numerous tesselated pavements and other remains of the Roman occupation, including the villa at the Barton, in Oakley Park. Many other works give admirable descriptions of Corinium, so that it seems only necessary to refer the reader to the following.

> See " Remains of Roman Art in Corinium," by Buckman.
> Also Rudder's " History of Gloucestershire," p. 343.
> Also "Archæological Journal," vol. vi., p. 321.
> Also "Archæologia," vol. xviii., p. 112.
> Also "Guide to the Corinium Museum," by Church.

No. 10.—DRYHILL VILLA.

This is situated half-a-mile north of Crickley Hill Camp, and three and a half miles south of Cheltenham. It was opened by Mr. W. H. Gomonde and Captain Bell about the year 1849. It consists of twelve rooms, and forms a great contrast to the Witcomb Villa three miles off. There are no tesselated pavements here, or any of the remnants of a rich man's dwelling. It was probably a *villa rustica*. The interior of the bath was lined with stucco several inches thick, of a reddish colour. The bath communicated with the hypocaust by means of a passage, with a solid floor laid with sandstone. The largest room measured 27 feet by 16 feet 8 inches. One portion of a brick was found with P R C stamped on it.

Underneath the floor of this room were large flues, arched over, dividing the chamber at right angles. The inside of the flues were full of charred wood and coal. A *crypto porticus* ran along the south-east side of the villa, and the wall between this and the north chamber was 120 feet in length, the breadth of the *porticus* being 6 feet 6 inches. One of the rooms, 20 feet by 16 feet, had been stuccoed and painted. The colours were green, blue, and various shades of red. Coins of Tetricus, Licinius, Crispus, Constantine, Valentinian, Valens, &c., were found ; also black, red, and white pottery, the handle of a glass bottle, a stylus of iron, knives, bronze fibulæ, perforated pieces of Kimmeridge coal, &c. I found large quantities of Roman pottery here in 1879, including sham Samian. No real Samian has been found.

See "Notes on Cheltenham, Ancient and Mediæval," by W. H. Gomonde, 1849.
Also " Transactions Bristol and Glou. Archæ. Soc.," 1879-80, p. 208.

No. 11.—Daglingworth Villa.

About the year 1690 the foundations of a Roman villa were discovered in the parish of Daglingworth, close to the Ermine Street, two and a half miles north-west of Cirencester. It was situated in a field called " Cave Close." I am not aware of any description of this, and am unable to give any details as to dimensions, or as to what articles of antiquity were found.

See Rudder's " History of Gloucestershire," p. 400.
Also Atkyn's "History of Gloucestershire," p. 198.
Also " Roman Antiquities at Woodchester," by S. Lysons, p. 19.

No. 12.—Dodington Villa.

Many Roman antiquities have been found in the parish of Dodington, two and a half miles south-east of Chipping Sodbury, including remains of a Roman villa. It lies within two miles of the very perfect Roman camp at Sodbury. In an old description of Dodington I find the following :—" Pottes exceeding finely nelyd and florished in the Romanes tymes diggid out of the growndes in the feldes of Dodington, also a yerthen pot with Romayne coins."

> See Rudder's "History of Gloucestershire," p. 412.
> Also Leland's "Itinerary," vol. vi., fol. 75.
> Also "Camden's Britannia," by Gough, p. 276.

No. 13.—GLEVUM.

The remarks made under the head of Corinium seem to apply to Glevum. It would be out of place to attempt a detailed description of the various Roman remains found at Gloucester. The object of this work is rather to call attention to those objects of antiquarian interest scattered far and wide throughout our county, and very little known to the majority of readers, than to dwell on the oft-told narrative of Roman remains in Corinium and Glevum.

> See all the Histories of Gloucestershire.
> Also " Proceedings Cott. Nat. Field Club," vol. vi., p. 154.
> Also "Archæologia," vol. x., p. 132.
> Also " The Celt, the Roman, and the Saxon," p. 161.
> Also " Gentleman's Magazine," vol. xl., p. 40.
> Also " Gentleman's Magazine," vol. xliii., p. 248.
> Also " Transactions Bristol and Glou. Archæ. Soc.," 1876, p. 153.
> Also " Transactions Bristol and Glou. Archæ. Soc.," 1877-78, p. 210.
> Also "Crania Britannica," vol. ii.

No. 14.—HARESFIELD VILLA.

This lies in the parish of Haresfield, in the hamlet of Stockend, five miles south of Gloucester. It is on the northeast side of Brodbro' Green, on a farm known as Brook's Farm, not far from the well known camp on Haresfield Beacon. It is situated by the side of Daniel's Brook, at a spot known as "Rudge Dowler," the existing boundary fence being the actual wall of the Roman villa. Large numbers of tesseræ have been found here, also two columns, which the tenant farmer converted into garden rollers. Mr. Niblett, in sending me a description of the villa, says :—" I myself dug in a place or two and found broken roof-tiles, flue-tiles, pottery, and coloured plaster ; also one solitary silver coin of Theodosius. For twelve years or so tons of stone had been carted away from the villa to mend the parish roads. Old Robert Davis said there was ' nout but a lot o' rubble, and it grew nothing but ettles, so he thought he would try and make a ground on it.' "

No. 15.—Kingscote Villa.

In the year 1691 the remains of a Roman villa were found in a field called the " Chestles," in the parish of Kingscote, four miles south-east of Dursley. A great number of Roman coins were discovered, also a large statue of stone and an ancient fibula vestiaria of brass, curiously chequered with red and blue enamel. The building itself contained at least one tesselated pavement.

See Rudder's " History of Gloucestershire," p. 512.
Also " Roman Antiquities at Woodchester," by S. Lyons, p. 19.

No. 16.—Lydney Villa.

This fine Roman building occupied a commanding position in Lydney Park, one mile west of the town. It was first investigated in the year 1805, by the Hon. C. Bathurst. It would appear from the extent of the buildings, the elegance of some of the pavements, the hypocausts, and the painted stuccoes, that it was the residence of an officer of high rank. The coins found here extend from Augustus to Arcadius, and this seems to point to the conclusion that the building was occupied during the whole period of the Roman dominion in Britain. The buildings, which stand within the large camp described under the head of "Ancient Camps," extended in a direction north and south, measuring in this direction 300 feet, and from east to west 315 feet. The rooms in general were small, the largest being 24 feet by 18 feet. They number no less than sixty-four, including passages ; this includes both the villa and temple. The latter, which stands in a courtyard south-west of the villa, measures 93 feet by 76 feet. It is believed to have been a temple from three inscriptions found in it, two of which were on bronze plates and the third on lead. These were evidently votive tablets; on each tablet the name of the god is spelt differently, first—Nodons; second, Nodens; third, Nudens. A large number of articles of bronze, iron, and bone were found; also several bracelets, knives, lamps, and a considerable quantity of Roman pottery. Over 700 coins found here are described in detail in Mr. Bathurst's work referred to below.

>See "Roman Antiquities at Lydney Park," by Rev. W. H. Bathurst.
>Also " Archæologia," vol. v., p. 208.
>Also "Antiquarian Repertory," vol i., p. 134.
>Also "Antiquarian Repertory," vol. ii., p. 389.
>Also "Proceedings Society of Antiq.," 2d. series, vol. v., p. 96.
>Also Rudder's "History of Gloucestershire," p. 525.

No. 17.—Painswick Villa.

Remains of a Roman villa have been found in the parish of Painswick, on a farm called Highfield, about half a mile north-west of the town. Walls were found, crossing one another at right angles; also many flue tiles, and some Roman coins. It was opened some years ago in a rough and hurried way, and covered up again. A short account of it appeared in the public press at the time.

No. 18.—Rodmarton Villa.

This lies in the parish of Rodmarton, six miles south-west of Cirencester, in a field called "Hockbury," a quarter of a mile north-east of the Church. It was first noticed in the year 1636, when the following entry appears in the parish register:—" Hoc anno in agris in loco Hocbery vocato dum sulcos aratro ducunt, discooperta sunt tesselata pavimenta, tegulæ quibus ferrei clavi infixi, subrutæ, nummi quoque ænei Antonini et Valentiniani Imp : Incolæ mihi dixeunt, se æneos et argenteos nummos sæpius ibidem reperiisse, nescientes quid rei essent : a patribus autem audivisse, Rodmarton ab illo loco translatam olim ubi nunc est positam esse, apparet autem stationem aliquam Romanorum ibidem aliquando fuisse." There is still a local tradition that the Church of Rodmarton was removed from Hockbury to its present site by the devil. In the year 1800 Mr. Lysons discovered a Roman villa consisting of thirteen rooms and passages. It was of small size, the space occupied by it being 86 feet by 41 feet. Three of the rooms had tesselated pavements; there was also a hypocaust. The foundation walls were of local stone, but a large number of bricks were used. Several of these were stamped with four letters, viz., T P F C, T P F A, T P F P.

See "Archæologia," vol. xviii., p. 113.
Also Rudder's "History of Gloucestershire," p. 631.

No. 19.—Stinchcombe Villa.

This is to be found in the parish of Stinchcombe, in the hamlet of Stancombe, about one mile west of Dursley. It lies on a bank opposite the late Mr. Purnell's house. Fragments of the tesselated pavement found in the villa are now in the Museum at Gloucester; also hair-pins and other trinkets, thoughtfully and kindly given to the establishment by Miss Purnell. In a letter from our learned antiquary, Mr. Niblett, he says:—"I distinctly remember the pitched road leading to this villa being very perfect, with two arms in the form of the letter Y."

No. 20.—Swell Villa.

This occupies high ground in the parish of Lower Swell, half a mile west of Stow-on-the-Wold. It was much disturbed about twenty years ago, when the tenant farmer built some sheds from the foundation walls of the villa and levelled up his farmyard with broken Roman pottery! An eye-witness who was present on the occasion narrates the following fact:—"There were tremendous, extraordinary foundations of great stones, several feet down, all in clay." Some of the rooms can still be traced. The *crypto porticus* is 8 feet wide, and then come three rooms—the first 45 feet by 12 feet, the second 33 feet by 12 feet, and the third 28 feet by 12 feet.

The old road, "Via Regia," runs in front of this villa, and immediately on the other side of the old road are the remains of a large room, 50 feet long. There is a good spring of water close to the villa, and at a little distance is an ancient kiln, which was found to be full of red ashes. A large brown jug of Roman pottery was found here, also flue-tiles, Roman coins, cockle shells, large quantities of burnt stone, &c. I had an opportunity of examining the foundations of the villa in December, 1881, when some further excavations were made for the purpose of finding tesselated pavements, but without success, pottery and coins being the only relics discovered.

No. 21.—Wadfield Villa.

This was discovered in 1863 on the Sudeley estate, about one and a half miles south of Winchcombe. It has been figured and described by Mrs. Dent in her valuable work, "Annals of Winchcombe and Sudeley." It consisted of about fourteen rooms and passages, and when found was in a perfect state of preservation. The dimensions of the rooms were about fifteen feet square, the hypocaust being situated at the south side of the villa. A beautiful tesselated pavement was discovered, and this is now carefully preserved in a greenhouse in the garden of Sudeley Castle. Among other articles found were some Roman rings, beads, a glass pendant, bronze fibula, portion of a statue, &c.; also several coins and portions of pottery.

See "Annals of Winchcombe and Sudeley," p. 13.

No. 22.—Witcomb Villa.

This was discovered in 1818 in a field called Sarendells, in the parish of Great Witcomb, five miles south-east of Gloucester. It is a building of great extent, thirty-four rooms and passages having been explored. It lies on sloping ground facing the south-east, near Cooper's Hill, well sheltered by the beech woods, and having a good supply of pure water (now forming part of the water supply of Gloucester). Many Roman coins, from the time of Constantine to that of Valentinian and Valens, have been found; and a great variety of articles, including a small steelyard (*statera*), with its weight attached; an ivory comb; a stone mortar six inches in diameter; and a ploughshare of iron weighing seven pounds, now in the British Museum; many fibulæ, buckles, and pins; and a British flint axe, five and a half inches long and two and a half inches broad. A passage six feet wide was discovered, leading by a descent of several steps to one of the main rooms. The walls of this were plastered and painted in panels, formed by stripes of light blue and orange colours on a white ground, having elegant ornaments of ivy leaves, &c., between them. In this passage were found Roman coins, many bones of animals, several skulls of bullocks, goats, &c., with fragments of stag's horn, and an iron axe. The set of Roman baths are very complete. Outside the sacrarium, a room appointed to sacred uses, was found the figure of a lyre cut in stone. The tesselated pavements are most interesting; that in one of the baths consists of nine octagonal departments, five of which enclosed circles, and in the centre of the pavement is the figure of an urn with ivy leaves. Another bath has a mosaic pavement, ornamented with figures of fish and sea monsters in blue on a white ground, enclosed within a border formed by a double fret. The Ermine Street, running between Gloucester and Cirencester, passes within three-quarters of a mile of the villa, and another Roman road, called the Sarn Way, is close at hand.

See "Archæologia," vol. xix., p. 178.
Also "Transactions Bristol and Glou. Archæ. Soc.," 1879-80, p. 34.
Also "Proceedings Cott. Nat. Field Club," vol. v., p. 247.

No. 23.—WITHINGTON VILLA.

This lies half a mile south of the village of Withington, six miles from Cheltenham. It was discovered in 1811 by Mr. H. C. Brooke. The remains lie 150 yards from the river Colne, and consist of fifteen rooms and passages. Eight of these had tesselated pavements. One is of great size, measuring 35 feet by 20 feet, and is a very fine specimen of mosaic work, Orpheus being in the centre surrounded by various animals. The villa, like many others in the neighbourhood, appears to have been consumed by fire, as the remains of burnt timber and melted lead were found in several places. Several portions of the pavements are now in the British Museum, a very fine one containing the head of Neptune. The part of the field in which the villa was found is called the Old Town, or Withington-upon-Wall Well, from a fine spring so named which rises near it. The walls of the building were mostly 1 foot 8 inches thick, of different heights up to four feet. They were all built of local stone, plastered on the inside, and painted with stripes of different colours. The eastern part of the building contained the hypocaust, the dimensions of which were 27 feet 6 inches by 19 feet.

See " Archæologia," vol. xviii., p. 18.

No. 24.—Woodchester Villa.

This celebrated Roman villa is situated in a charming valley about two miles south-west of Stroud, and the same distance north-west of Nailsworth. It consists of no less than sixty-four rooms, thirty-seven of which are ranged round a courtyard or quadrangle which measures 92 feet by 93 feet. It was examined by that great antiquary, Mr. Samuel Lysons, in the year 1793. The largest pavement formed a square of 48 feet 10 inches, and is superior to any other tesselated pavement found in Great Britain. The general design of it is a circular area 25 feet in diameter, enclosed in a square frame consisting of twenty-four compartments. The large circular compartment is surrounded by a border consisting of a Vitrurian scroll edged on each side by a guilloche, and enriched with foliage proceeding from a mask of Pan having a beard of leaves; immediately within the border are representations of various beasts, originally twelve in number, on a white ground, including a gryphon, a bear, a leopard, a stag, a tigress, a lion, a lioness, a boar, a dog, and an elephant. Most of these figures are about four feet in length. Within this circle is a smaller one, with various birds on a white ground, also a fox. Within the circle of birds is an octagonal compartment, in the south side of which are openings to admit the principal figure of the design. It represents Orpheus playing on the lyre, which he rests on his left knee. In the four angular spaces between the border of the pavement and the great circular compartment are the remains of female figures, two of which appear to have been in each of those spaces. This pavement had several flues running underneath it, which crossed each other at right angles. These are 4 feet high, and 1 foot 11 inches wide at the bottom. The remains of tesselated pavements were found in ten other compartments. The villa included in its arrangements a hypocaust, a laconicum or sweating room, a præfurnium, and a crypto porticus which was 114 feet long. Among the articles found here may be mentioned the following :—Fragments of stucco, painted in fresco ; fragments of foreign marble ; fragments of statuary, pottery, and glass ; portions of a white marble group of Cupid and Psyche; portions of stags' horns ; several human bones ; coins of Hadrian, Lucella, Tetricus, Victorinus, Probus, Constantinus, Constantius, Crispus, Valentinus, and Valens ; a stone weight, weighing thirteen and a half pounds ; a circular trough of stone three feet in diameter ; knives, daggers, hatchet of brass, spurs of iron, fibulæ, pins, &c.

See " Roman Antiquities Discovered at Woodchester," by Lysons.
Also Atkyn's " History of Gloucestershire."
Also King's " Munimenta Antiqua," vol. ii., p. 185.
Also Rudder's " History of Gloucestershire," p. 841.
Also "Camden's Britannia," by Gough, p. 275.

No. 25.—WYCOMB.

This is in the parish of Whittington, close to Andoversford, and five miles from Cheltenham. It was in all probability the site of a British village, and afterwards of an important

Roman military station, combined with residential houses and villas. The area of Wycomb as far as examined is 25 acres, and over the whole of this foundations have been discovered. Roman coins have been found in very large quantities. The track of a road was distinctly visible on the north-east side, and at the end of this road were two masses of buildings, intersected by a wall of cut masonry 145 feet long, running at right angles to the road. A room on the north side of the wall measured 45 feet 6 inches by 22 feet, with other walls and pavements adjoining it. The floors were mostly of stone, laid in cement and ground concrete. Pottery has been found in immense quantities, including good specimens of plain and figured Samian. Several good fibulæ, styli, sacrificial and other knives, keys, articles of toilet, and a beautiful bronze statuette three inches in height, were also found. All these objects of interest were kindly lent by Mrs. Lawrence, of Sevenhampton, for exhibition at the temporary museum formed in Cheltenham on the occasion of the Bristol and Gloucestershire Archæological Society's meeting on January 19th, 1881. No position could have been better suited for the concentration of troops than Wycomb. It lies in a fertile and sheltered valley, adjoining an abundant supply of pure water, and close to the roads leading to the strongly fortified camps on the hill tops in every direction.

See "Gentleman's Magazine," November, 1863, p. 627.
Also "Gentleman's Magazine," January, 1864, p. 86.
Also "Transactions Bristol and Glou. Archæ. Soc.," 1879-80, p. 209.

No. 26.—SPOONLY VILLA.

In March, 1882, a fine Roman Villa was accidently discovered in Spoonly Wood, on the Sudeley Castle Estate, three miles from Winchcombe. A workman who was employed in making a road, on moving a large stone, found a tesselated pavement within a few inches of the surface; this proved to be a floor raised on pilæ, and approached from the lower level by a flight of five steps. At the time of writing, eighteen rooms and passages have been explored, but these do not comprise half the total number. Traces of the walls can be seen covering an area of 200 feet by 140 feet. Six tesselated pavements have already been found, some of them of great beauty. A large amount of pottery, mostly broken, numbers of roofing tiles, floor tiles, stone columns, a few Roman coins, and various other articles—including spoons—have been found. In a room near the south-east corner is a Roman well, about thirteen feet deep and two feet nine inches in diameter; this was filled up with earth, but shortly after it was cleared out a good supply of water flowed in. In the same room are two stones, two feet nine inches high, standing on end, the distance between them being two feet four inches, and near these stones were found the remnants of two querns for grinding purposes. Outside this room, in the corridor, which has a tesselated pavement, stand a basement of flat stones measuring seven feet by six feet; these stones stand upon the tesselated pavement. Until this most interesting Roman Villa is further explored it is impossible to enter into greater detail. Fortunately, it has fallen into good hands. Under the care of Mr. and Mrs. Dent we may hope to see a Roman Villa preserved as it ought to be.

END OF VILLAS.

LONG BARROWS.

No. 1.—ABLINGTON BARROW.

This is situated in the parish of Ablington, about three and a half miles south of Northleach. It was opened in the year 1854. Direction, north and south; its length is about 270 feet, and greatest width 100 feet; its height at the northern end being twelve feet. It is composed of the common oolitic stone of the country. Unlike other barrows in the county, it is surrounded by a double wall of masonry, each having a face outwards and filled with rubble. Towards the north, these walls make a double curve inwards, and in the centre of this curve, between the two walls, stands a large stone, six feet high and five feet wide. An interment was found near the north end of the tumulus in a grave made of rough stones; a few worked flints were also found, but the barrow has never been thoroughly examined. Adjoining the barrow are the remains of a round hut built underground, formed of dry walling similar in character to that found in the tumulus.

See "Our British Ancestors," 1865, p. 318.
Also "Flint Chips," p. 494.
Also "Anthropological Review," vol. iii., p. 71.

No. 2.—AVENING BARROW.

This lies half a mile to the east of the village of Avening, and two and a half miles from Nailsworth. It is 160 feet long, its greatest width being 60 feet, and greatest height 6 feet. Its direction is east and west, the highest portion of the barrow being at the east end. It was opened in the year 1809 by the

Rev. N. Thornbury, Rector of Avening. Three stone chambers were taken out and removed to a grove in the rectory garden, where they are carefully preserved.

See "Archæologia," vol. xvi., p. 362.
Also "Proceedings Cott. Nat. Field Club," vol. v., p. 280.

No. 3.—BELAS KNAPP.

This celebrated barrow is situated in the parish of Charlton Abbots, seven miles east of Cheltenham and four from Winchcombe, just above a wood known as "Humble Bee How," or "Humble Bey How." It is 197 feet long, and 75 feet wide near the centre, its greatest height being twelve feet six inches. Its direction is north and south, the highest part of the barrow being at the north end. A wall of dry stone surrounded the barrow about two feet high except at the north end, where it rose to seven feet and curved inwards, so as to form a passage towards the centre. This ended about twenty feet from the outer slope in a massive slab set vertically between two pillars, and supporting a still larger slab set horizontally. At the sides of the barrow are two smaller openings leading to cells, and another cell or cist is towards the southern end. In 1863 a large flat stone, lying exposed on the surface of the barrow at its southern end, was removed, and proved to be the cover of a cell six feet long and two feet six inches wide. In this were found four human bodies, some bones and tusks of boars, a bone scoop, four pieces of pottery, and a few flints. In the autumn of 1863 five more bodies of children and one young man were found at the north end, under a stone eight feet square and two feet thick. Another chamber was found in 1864 on the east side; it was formed of four large rough stones, enclosing an area about five feet square. In this, twelve skeletons were found, but no pottery or flints. Another cist was found at the south end covered with three large horizontal stones, and walled all round. Another chamber was found on the west side containing the remains of no less than fourteen bodies. The number of skeletons found altogether numbered thirty-eight, of all ages, from the infant to extreme old age. All the skulls were of the dolicho-cephalic type except one, and this was doubtless from a secondary interment.

See " Proceedings Soc. Ant.," 2nd ser., vol. iii., p. 275.
Also "Mem. Anthrop. Soc." vol. i., p. 474.
Also " Proceedings Cott. Nat. Field Club," vol. vi., p. 337.

No. 4.—Bisley Barrow.

A long barrow was opened in 1863 a little to the south of Bisley. A short account of it appeared in the local papers at the time, but I have been unable to find it. The barrow has since been entirely destroyed.

See " Archæologia," vol. xlii., p. 201.

No. 5.—Bown Hill Barrow.

This lies on Bown Hill, above Woodchester, three miles south-west of Stroud, and two miles north-west of Nailsworth. It is 180 feet long, its greatest width being 50 feet. Its direction is east-north-east and west-south-west, the highest end being towards the east-north-east. It was opened by the Cotteswold Naturalists' Field Club in May, 1863. The interior of the barrow was constructed of angular masses of stone, heaped together without any order, amongst which were scattered blocks of considerable size. Only one chamber was found; this was formed of five large stones, two on each side and one placed transversely, measuring eight feet six inches by four feet. The remains of six skeletons were found, and several bones of cattle, teeth of the horse and ox, several boars' tusks, a small flint flake, and some pieces of rude pottery. The barrow had evidently been previously disturbed, and this fact will probably account for the presence of a brass coin of the Roman Emperor Germanicus.

See "Proceedings Cott. Nat. Field Club," vol. iii., p 199.
Also " Proceedings Cott. Nat. Field Club," vol. v., p. 279.

Nos. 6 and 7.—CAMP BARROWS.

There are two interesting long barrows a little to the south of the village of Camp, two miles north of Bisley; they have been previously described as round barrows, but such is not the case. They are situated close together, the "horned" ends being only 15 feet apart; they extend in contrary directions, one towards the north, the other towards the south. The dimensions of the southern barrow are as follow:—Length, 130 feet; greatest width, 90 feet; the "horned" end being towards the north. The circumscribing walls, formed of Stonefield slate, are exposed to view in a quarry at the southern end. The northern barrow measures 150 feet by 74 feet, the "horned" end being towards the south. There are four large stones visible in this barrow, forming a chamber. A great number of human skeletons have at various times been dug up near the village of Champ. No fortifications are now to be seen here to account for the name, but there is a local tradition that there was a Danish camp in the neighbourhood.

No. 8.—CIRENCESTER BARROW.

There is a long barrow in the "Querns" field, close to the Cirencester Railway Station, on the south-west of the town; its length is about 180 feet. It was opened thirty years ago by Messrs. Newmarsh and Buckman, and is mentioned by them in their "Remains of Roman Art in Cirencester." It is there suggested that the word "querns" is derived from "cairn," or burial place. The Roman amphitheatre lies a little to the south-east end of the barrow. Several skeletons were found arranged east and west, but it seems they were in a very fragmentary state, none of them being in a condition to be capable of measurement. The explorations consisted simply of two transverse cuts through the mound, so that it is impossible to say what may yet be found.

See Buckman's "Corinium," p. 12.

LONG BARROWS.

Nos. 9 and 10.—CRICKLEY BARROWS (Nos. 1 and 2).

There are two long barrows at Crickley Barrow, two miles south of Northleach, adjoining the ancient Salt Way, but as far as I know they have never been examined or described, and, without a thorough exploration with pick-axe and shovel, it would be impossible to say anything definite about them.

No. 11.—CRIPPETTS BARROW.

This fine tumulus is a conspicuous object on Shurdington Hill, three miles south of Cheltenham, and three quarters of a mile north-east of the Crickley Hill Camp. The position affords extensive views over the vale of Gloucester. The barrow is 189 feet long, its greatest width being 100 feet, and greatest height 20 feet. Its direction is nearly east and west, the highest position lying towards the east. Many years ago the tenant of the land began to move away part of the earth at the southern extremity, and in doing so uncovered a cromlech, in which was found a skeleton and several articles of which no satisfactory account can now be obtained. The ground in which the tumulus stands is still called the "Barrow Piece." It has never been thoroughly examined, though it has been carefully protected by placing a fence round it—a good example which might be followed in many other cases. There are two round barrows in the same field.

See "Journal of Archæological Association," vol. iii., p. 64.
Also "Celt, Roman, and Saxon," 1875, p. 74.
Also "Anthropological Review," vol. iii., pp. 66 and 71.
Also "Archæologia," vol. xlii., p. 201.

No. 12.—DUNTISBOURNE BARROW.

There are two high circular mounds in Cherry Wood, near Duntisbourne Heath, five miles north-west of Cirencester, which have always been considered round barrows. Through the kindness of Lord Bathurst I superintended some excavations there this year (1882), and discovered that the two mounds formed the ends of a huge long barrow, having a total length of 210 feet. The central portion of the tumulus must have been removed ages back. The circumscribing wall is in a good state of preservation on the south side. The direction of the barrow is nearly east and west. Further examination will, I hope, enable me to give a fuller description of this very interesting pre-historic monument at a future time. During the late excavation one very perfectly formed flint scraper was found, and several small bones. Part of the outside wall at the west end was removed a few years back, but no interments have yet been found. There are several round barrows in the immediate neighbourhood, and Pinbury Camp is only one mile distant on the south.

No. 13.—Edgworth Barrow.

This barrow lies three-quarters of a mile north-west of the village of Edgworth, and two miles east of Bisley. I have not heard of any excavation or exploration having been made, but I mention it here as one of the Gloucestershire long barrows.

No. 14.—Eyford Barrow.

This lies in the parish of Eyford, three miles from Stow-on-the-Wold. Its length is 108 feet, its greatest width being 44 feet, and greatest height three feet six inches, though it was probably much higher. Its direction is east-north-east and west-south-west. The interior of the barrow consisted of oolitic rubble and slabs, and it was surrounded by a wall of thin Stonefield slates. At the east end it assumed the "horned" form, the north-eastern horn being narrower and longer than the other. Four chambers were discovered, one of which contained six human skeletons and one dog's skeleton lying *in situ*, also scattered bones of the ox and sheep. This chamber was situated eighty feet from the east end, and measured five feet six inches by four feet. In another chamber, seven feet eight inches in length, were found the remains of ten bodies, and close in front of the neck of one of the bodies—that of a woman—was a bead or amulet, composed of kimmeridge shale or similar substance. The bead is slightly oval in outline and much flattened ; the perforation has been made from both ends and is very wide, having, no doubt, been made with a flint borer. I call especial attention to this bead, as it was the first ornament ever discovered in connection with a primary interment in a long barrow ; and it is a remarkable fact that the only ornament I have discovered in a long barrow is of precisely the same character (see Notgrove Barrow). Other skeletons were found and various portions of pottery.

See " British Barrows," p. 514.
Also "Jour. Anthrop. Inst.," vol. v., p. 120.

No. 15.—Giant's Stone Barrow.

This is in the parish of Bisley, one mile east of the village. The barrow has been removed, or nearly so, leaving some of the stones which formed the chambers, especially a large one locally known as the Giant's Stone. There are many hundred suspicious-looking depressions adjoining the barrow, which are supposed by many to be ancient pit-dwellings.

No. 16.—Hasleton Barrow (No 1).

This lies on the top of the Cotteswold hills, in the parish of Hasleton, four miles north-west of Northleach, in a field known as the Barrow Ground, and close to the ancient Salt Way. Its length is 150 feet, greatest width 70 feet, and present height about five feet ; but originally it must have been more than double this height. Its direction is north-west and south-east, the highest part being towards the south-east. The top of two upright stones, evidently forming sides of a chamber, are visible on the surface of the ground near the south-east end ; they lie parallel to each other and ten feet apart. One stone measures on the top one foot six inches by five inches ; the other, two feet by five inches ; but it is impossible to say what height they are without excavation. I found several worked flakes on the surface of the barrow, and I have heard of others being found since. The barrow has evidently been much damaged by the plough, but has not, I think, ever been examined. The interior is composed of oolitic slabs and Stonesfield slate.

No. 17.—Hasleton Barrow (No. 2).

In the same field as the last, and only eighty yards from it, is another long barrow, the original length of which must have been about 174 feet ; greatest width, 78 feet ; its present height being 9 feet. Its direction is east and west, the highest part being towards the east. The interior is composed of stone similar to the last. I found a well-worked flint flake on the surface. This barrow has never been thoroughly examined, though many stones have been removed for road making and wall building.

No. 18.—Hoar Stone Tumulus.

This lies in the parish of Duntisbourn Abbots, about four and a half miles from Cirencester. It was 120 feet long and 90 feet wide, composed of loose quarry stones. The largest stone at the east end has been long known by the name of the " Hoar Stone ;" it is of the calcareous kind, twelve feet high, thirteen feet in circumference, and weighs between five and six tons; it was half above and half under ground. Another stone, about nine feet square and one foot thick, lay flat on the ground ; this covered a chamber in which the remains of eight or nine human bodies were discovered. The chamber was divided into two cells about four feet square and six feet deep.

See " Archæologia," vol. xvi., p. 362.
Also " Gentleman's Magazine," vol. lxxvi., p. 971.

No. 19.—Idols Barrow.

I have lately been informed that there is a long barrow in Pope's Wood, near Prinknash Park, about four and a half miles south-east of Gloucester, known as "Idol's Barrow." It lies close to the ancient Portway, but I have not had an opportunity of examining the mound with the care necessary to say any thing definite on the subject.

No. 20.—LECHMORE BARROW.

This lies one and half miles south of Nailsworth. It is 120 feet long, 65 feet wide, and six feet high ; its direction is east and west, the highest part being towards the east. It has been much disturbed at various times. In 1812 one chamber still remained, but the stones of which it was constructed have since been removed for building material, and the mound itself is now reduced in size year by year by the operation of the plough.

See "Proceedings Cott. Nat. Field Club," vol. v., p. 280.

No. 21.—LEIGHTERTON BARROW.

This is situated in the parish of Boxwell, six and a half miles west of Tetbury ; it is locally known as " West Barrow," and was opened about the year 1700 by Matthew Huntley. It contained three vaults arched over like ovens, and at the entrance of each was found an earthen jar containing burnt human bones, but the skulls and thigh-bones were found unburnt.

See Atkyn's " History of Gloucestershire," p. 155.
Also Rudder's " History of Gloucestershire," p. 306.

No. 22.—LITTLETON DREW BARROW.

This was first noticed by John Aubrey in his MS., " Monumenta Britannica," in the seventeenth century ; it was called " Lugbury." It lies in the parish of Nettleton, but close to Littleton Drew, in Wiltshire, just outside the boundary of our county. It measures 180 feet in length, and 90 feet in breadth, its greatest elevation being six feet. Its direction is nearly due east and west. There are three stones at the east end, on the slope of the barrow, thirty feet from its base ; the two uprights are six feet six inches apart, two feet thick, and four feet wide ; one is six feet six inches high, the other five feet six inches. Resting on the mound and leaning againt the uprights is a large stone, twelve feet long, six feet wide, and two feet thick. A cist was discovered about sixty feet from the east end, containing one skeleton. Another cist was found on the south side. Three other cists were also found, about ten feet long, four feet wide, and two feet deep, formed of rough stone. The total number of skeletons found numbered twenty-six. Several flint flakes were also discovered.

See "Crania Britannica," vol. ii.
Also " Ancient Wilts," vol. ii., p. 99 (Hoar).
Also " History of Castle Combe," p. 7 (Scrope).

No. 23.—LODGE PARK BARROW.

There is a fine long barrow in Sherborne Lodge Park, two miles south-east of Northleach ; its length is about 150 feet, and greatest width 70 feet. Some of the stones forming the chambers are visible on the surface. Its direction is south-east and north-west, the highest portion lying towards the south-east. No examination has ever been made of the mound.

No. 24.—NOTGROVE BARROW.

This interesting barrow is situated in the " Poor's Lots," one mile north-west of the village of Notgrove, and close to the new Railway Station on the Banbury and Cheltenham line. I examined it in April, 1881, previous to a visit of the Cotteswold Field Club. I found the barrow was 140 feet long, and that its greatest width was 78 feet. The entire crown of the tumulus had at some time been removed, exposing to view twenty large stones ; these formed a series of chambers of the double-cruciform type, similar to those at Uley and Nymphs-field. On reference to the ground plan on the margin of the

LONG BARROWS. 83

map, it will be seen that there is a central passage with two chambers on each side. The passage is five feet wide towards the south-east end, and four feet three inches wide towards the north-west, its entire length being twenty-seven feet. The first chamber on the west measures eight feet four inches by six feet; the second measures six feet four inches by six feet; chamber No. 3, somewhat different in shape, measured six feet across in each direction; and chamber No. 4, nine feet six inches by seven feet. The largest stone stands five feet above the original surface of the ground, being three feet long and sixteen inches wide. Chamber No. 4 had never been disturbed, though the other three had been cleared of their contents in past ages. Under a large flat stone I discovered portions of two human skeletons, lying in a contracted position; the skulls, which were lying towards the west, were broken into very small pieces. With these human remains were found two teeth and the pelvis of some kind of ox (probably *Bos longifrons*), a dog's tooth, a very perfect leaf-shaped arrow-head of flint, a black oval bead or amulet one and a half inches long, composed of kimmeridge shale, having a hole pierced through the centre by a flint borer (this bead, though larger, resembles the one found in the Eyford Long Barrow, described in "British Barrows," page 519); lastly, thirty pieces of rough British pottery, half baked and belonging to the same vessel, one piece only showing the form of the rim. The spaces between the upright stones in chamber No. 4 were filled up with well-built dry walls of Stonesfield slate; the bottom of the chamber was paved with small flat stones well fitted together and forming a level surface.

No. 25.—Nymphsfield Barrow.

This is situated on the escarpment of the Cotteswold Hills, in the parish of Nymphsfield, on an eminence known as Crawley Hill, half a mile north of the barrow at Uley, and two miles north-east of Dursley. It was examined by the

Cotteswold Field Club in 1862. Its length was 120 feet, and greatest breadth 85 feet; its direction was east and west, the highest part being towards the east. Twenty-four upright stones were discovered forming a central passage, with a double set of cruciform chambers on either side almost identical in dimensions to those at Uley and Notgrove; in one of these was partitioned off a smaller chamber or cist, probably for the remains of an infant found therein. In some parts the spaces between the upright stones were filled up with dry walling. The remains of sixteen human skeletons were found, also some bones of the ox, hog, dog, and birds, a few fragments of pottery, and some flint flakes. All the skulls were of pronounced dolicho-cephalic type.

See "Journal Anthrop. Soc.," vol. iii., p. 66.
Also " Proceedings Cott. Nat. Field Club," vol. iii., p. 184.
Also " Transactions Bristol and Glou. Archæ. Soc.," vol. v., p. 95.

No. 26.—Randwick Barrow.

This lies on the top of Randwick Hill, a quarter of a mile from the village of Randwick, and two miles north-west of Stroud; it is 150 feet long, its greatest width being 86 feet, and greatest height 13 feet; its direction is east and west, the highest part being towards the east. It is composed of oolitic rubble and slabs, and is enclosed by a well-built wall formed of thin stones; this wall is exposed in two places on the west side, where a portion of the barrow has been destroyed by quarrying operations. The stones of the interior are for the most part laid at an angle of 45 degrees, overlapping one another. At the east end it appears to have two well-developed "horns." On visiting the barrow in March, 1881, I found a portion of a human tibia, much stained with manganic oxide and black fungus. There are two round barrows within a few hundred yards, and some earthworks cutting off the neck of the hill, thus forming a camping ground. The three barrows are within the defended area.

No. 27.—RODMARTON BARROW.

This was opened by Mr. Lysons in 1863 it lies; within half a mile of the village of Rodmarton, and was known by the popular name of "Windmill Tump." It is 176 feet long, 71 feet wide, and ten feet high; its direction was east and west, the widest end being towards the east. A few feet below the surface of the east end two very large stones were found standing upright, each of them eight feet six inches in height; against these was leaning a third stone of vast size, in a slanting position. A chamber was found on the north side formed of seven large upright stones, with a paved floor, covered at the top by a single stone measuring nine feet by eight feet, and eighteen inches thick. The chamber was approached by a narrow passage, with walls on either side. Within the chamber were found no less than thirteen skeletons, also five flint arrow-heads, a large piece of natural flint, and some coarse black pottery. Another chamber was discovered on the southern side, much of the same character, but composed of nine stones instead of seven.

See "Archæologia," vol. ix., p. 367.
Also "Our British Ancestors" (Lysons), p. 137.
Also "Reliq. Brit. Rom.," vol. ii., p. 8.
Also "Reliq. Brit. Rom.," vol. iii., p. 7.
Also "Proc. Soc. Ant.," 2nd ser., vol. ii., p. 275.
Also "Crania Brit.," vol. ii.

No. 28.—SELSLEY HILL BARROW.

This barrow is generally known as "The Toots," and is situated high up on Selsley Hill, two miles south-west of Stroud. Its length is 210 feet, its greatest width 90 feet, and height 11 feet; its direction is east-north-east and west-south-west, the highest part lying towards the east-north-east. From these dimensions it will be seen that this is one of the largest long barrows in Gloucestershire. It has been opened in three places, but, unfortunately, no record has been preserved of the results of these excavations.

See "Proceedings Cott. Nat. Field Club," vol. v., p. 279.

No. 29.—SWELL BARROW (No. 1).

This barrow is situated in a field called "Cow Common," in the parish of Lower Swell, two and a half miles from the village, and three miles from Stow-on-the-Wold. Its length was about 150 feet, greatest width 77 feet, and greatest height five feet; its direction is east-south-east and west-north-west. It is entirely composed of slabs and rubble, and is surrounded by a carefully constructed wall of Stonesfield slate; this wall was two feet three inches high on the south side. The chief chamber was on the north side, fifty-five feet from the east end, and was discovered by the Rev. David Royce in 1867. The sides of the chamber were constructed of large upright stones, one being three feet six inches by two feet four inches, the chamber itself being three feet square. It contained three skeletons, and to the south-west of it five other skeletons were found. The chamber had a passage leading to it from the surrounding wall. Another chamber was found thirty feet from the east end, measuring six feet by four feet eight inches, of an oval form; it contained bones of two adults and one infant, two flint flakes, several fragments of pottery, &c. This barrow assumed the "horned" shape at the east end. There are eight round barrows in the same field.

See "Jour. Anat. and Phys.," vol. iii., p. 252.
Also "Jour. Anthrop. Inst., vol. v., p. 120.
Also "British Barrows," p. 513.

No. 30.—SWELL BARROW (No. 2).

This is in the parish of Upper Swell, half a mile from the village, and one and a half miles from Stow-on-the-Wold. Its length was 173 feet, its greatest width 57 feet, and greatest height eight feet six inches; its direction was east by north and west by south, the highest portion lying towards the east. Like the others in this neighbourhood it is composed of oolitic rubble and slabs, and is surrounded by a wall, which at the east end reached to a height of five feet, and here it assumed the "horned" shape. Only one chamber was found in the whole

LONG BARROWS. 87

of this mound; this was twenty-four feet from the west end, and on the north side of the barrow; it had a passage leading to it similar to the last. The chamber was seven feet long, four feet wide, and three feet eight inches high. At least nine skeletons were found here, together with bones of the goat or sheep, ox, pig, and two pieces of pottery. In the passage were found three other skeletons. Near the surface of the barrow three bodies were discovered, evidently Saxons, as proved by the articles found with them, viz., two bronze buckles, an iron knife, and an amber bead.

See "Jour. Anthrop. Inst.," vol. v., p. 120.
Also "British Barrows," p. 521.

No. 31.—SWELL BARROW (No. 3).

This is in the parish of Upper Swell, half a mile west-south-west of the village, and the same distance north of Lower Swell. The extreme length was 120 feet, and extreme width 40 feet; its direction was north-north-east and south-south-west, its horned end being at the north-north-east end; its greatest height was five feet. It was surrounded by a wall which measured four feet in height at the north end. The principal interment was in a trench about twenty-eight feet long, six feet four inches wide, and two feet deep, and this was sunk below the original surface of the ground, similar to the trench described under the "West Tump." In this trench-chamber were found nineteen skeletons, also bones of the roe deer, red deer, ox, wild boar, goat, pig, &c., bone implements, one vessel of coarse pottery, and a considerable number of worked flints. Three Saxon skeletons were found near the surface of the barrow.

See "Jour. Anthrop. Inst.," vol. v., p. 120.
Also "British Barrows," p. 524.

No. 32.—THROUGHAM BARROW.

This barrow lies in Througham Field, one mile north of the village of Bisley. It is 100 feet long, its greatest width being 50 feet, and height five feet; its direction is east and west, the highest portion being towards the east. The mound was cut in two about fifty years ago to make room for a cottage and some pigstyes; the latter now occupy the centre of the barrow! During the excavation one human skeleton was found. Probably this is the only instance in the county of a prehistoric burial place being turned into a pigstye!

No. 33.—TINGLESTONE BARROW.

This lies near Gatcombe Park, half a mile north of the village of Avening, and one and a half miles from Minchinhampton. It is 130 feet long, 70 feet wide, and six feet high; its direction is north and south, the highest part being towards the north. It does not occupy, as the others do, the highest ground in the locality, for although it stands on a slight knoll it is overlooked from rising ground on its eastern side. It is also peculiar as being a crowned barrow. On the broadest portion of the mound stands a large stone six feet in height, which bears the name of the " Tingle Stone."

> See "Proceedings Cott. Nat. Field Club," vol. v., p. 280.
> Also Bigland's " Gloucestershire," p. 92.
> Also " Flint Chips," p. 494.

No. 34.—ULEY BARROW.

This is one of the most remarkable of the chambered tumuli in England; it is situated on the bold escarpment of the Cotteswold Hills, two miles north-west of Dursley, and only half a mile north of the celebrated camp known as " Uley Bury." This barrow is locally called " Hetty Pegley's Tump," from the Welsh "twmp" or "twmpath," a mound. It was discovered in the year 1820, when the beech trees which grew on it were cut down, and it was examined in February, 1821. The barrow is 120 feet in length, and 85 feet at its greatest width, its height being ten feet at the east end, where it is both higher and broader than at the west. It was at the east end, where it assumed the horned shape, that the entrance to a chamber was found. The outside walls of the barrow here turn in, forming a kind of passage leading to the entrance, which is formed by a trilithon composed of a large flat stone upwards of eight feet in length and four feet six inches deep, supported by two upright stones, leaving a space of only thirty inches below the lower edge of the large stone and the natural ground. On passing this entrance a gallery appears, twenty-two feet long, four feet six inches wide, and five feet high. Four chambers lead out of this gallery—two on each side; their form is somewhat irregular, and their dimensions about four feet six inches by four feet. The dry walling ran completely round the barrow. At the east end there were two walls running parallel to one another, and at the west end are several dry walls intersecting each other at right angles. The remains of nearly thirty skeletons were found during the excavations, but only two of the skulls (dolicho-cephalic in type) have been preserved. There was a secondary interment in the highest part of the barrow, within six inches of the surface; this, doubtless, belonged to the Roman Age, as three Roman coins were found.

See "Archæological Journal," vol. xi., p. 315.
Also "Archæologia," vol. xlii., p. 201.
Also "Crania Britannica," vol. ii.
Also "Transactions Bristol and Glou. Archæ. Soc.," vol. v., p. 86.

No. 35.—WEST TUMP.

This barrow is to be found in the middle of Buckholt Wood, in the parish of Brimpsfield, about one and a half miles south-west of Birdlip. I discovered it accidentally in July, 1880, and in the following autumn thoroughly examined it. The direction of the barrow is south-east and north-west, the well-developed " horns " being at the south-east end. Its length is 149 feet, greatest width 76 feet, and greatest height ten feet three inches. A well-built dry wall surrounds the whole mound, faced only on the outer side. At the south-east end, between the " horns," the walls attain a height of three feet six inches. The " horns " are of equal size, and in the centre of the concavity between them are two upright stones, forming, as it were, a doorway, but this proved to be a deception, as there was no passage or chamber at this end. Four skeletons were found lying outside the circumscribing wall and close to it. The principal chamber was discovered at a distance of eighty-two feet from the southern " horn." Here there was a passage through the wall two feet wide. In breaking through the rubble of the opening we found two pieces of British pottery and a very perfect leaf-shaped arrow-head. A passage, three feet wide and seven feet long, led to the main chamber or trench; this passage was filled with rubble and bones in a very disorderly and confused state. The chamber was excavated below the original surface of the ground, beginning gradually to decline until it reached a depth of fifteen inches. The width of it was four feet, and length fifteen feet six inches. We discovered the remains of upwards of twenty skeletons; the last one we found was at the end of the chamber, 24 feet from the outside wall; here were five flat stones, arranged in the shape of a semicircle, and on these was deposited in a contracted form the skeleton of, probably, a young female, with the remains of a baby in close proxmity. Professor Rolleston (whose valuable assistance I was privileged to have during the excavation) was of opinion that the barrow was erected in honour of this Cotteswold Chieftainess. All the skulls found were of the dolicho-cephalic type.

The following letter from Professor Rolleston was, I believe, the last he wrote on any archæological subject, and as it is of much interest to all antiquaries, I reproduce it in full, though it appeared with my Paper on this subject in the Proceedings of the Gloucestershire Archæological Society :—

"Hotel de Londres, Genoa, January 17th, 1881.

"My dear Mr. Witts,—As I shall not be able to be present at the meeting at Cheltenham, before which the discoveries you have made at the Cranham Long Barrow will be brought, I should like to put on paper some of the larger points which my opportunities for seeing the barrow

LONG BARROWS.

have impressed upon me. I am very sorry not to be present at your meeting, but, *per contra*, I am very glad to have seen so much of the explorations as by your kindness I did see; I regret also not to have been able to give a detailed account of the objects of interest, or at least of the bones found in the barrow; but, *per contra* again, the bones have been preserved and properly cared for, and having lasted to tell their own tale for some thousands (I do not say how many as yet) of years, they will well last a few more months now that they have been thus looked to. The first great point which your "West Tump" Barrow presents to my view, at least in the distant perspective into which my temporary exile puts me, is its freedom from any ambiguity or question as to its age. There is no room whatever for supposing that the tumulus itself is of any but a very early prehistoric age, or that the human bones which it contained *could* have belonged to men of the times of Cromwell, of Henry VI., or Henry IV., or to any metal-weaponed warriors, whether *Plantagenet, Saxon, Roman*, or *British*. How is this to be proved? The absence of any scrap of metal is, it may be said, only a negative argument towards the positive conclusion that the "West Tump" is a prehistoric tump. I should answer to this, that there is no cubical mass belonging to a metallic period and of equal bulk to this one, in which many scraps of metal could not be found. Notably in burial-grounds cast-off pans, as well as shards of pottery, are always to be found. I was struck, indeed, with the emphasis laid in a letter published recently in the "Times," as to the neglected state of a London cemetery, upon the shabby appearance presented by the flotsam and jetsam, into which metallic articles entered largely. But there is a much stronger argument for its prehistoric character than this, and it lies in the peculiar shape and conformation of the tump. The "West Tump" is a "horned cairn," and horned cairns are found all over Great Britain, from Caithness in the extreme north of Scotland, to the Peninsular of Gower in the extreme west of Wales. Now the peculiarities of a "horned cairn" are such, that it is impossible to imagine that they do not indicate to us that one race of men, and one only, must have combined them as they are combined. But we have no *record* of Great Britain having ever been so occupied by one single race in historic times; hence this tumulus is prehistoric.—Q.E.D. Think further of the distance and difficulty of inter-communication which even now separates Caithness from Cheltenham, and think what is implied in the view, that the same race of men must have spread from one spot to the other. There is yet another consideration which tells in favour of the prehistoric character of these tumps, and of their being prehistoric in a sense in which no other raised burial-place can claim to be. Their conformation appears to me to be modelled upon that of a limestone promontory burrowed into by water, and so hollowed into the caves which were the first dwelling-places of Troglodytic men. The houses of the dead have in many places and in all ages been modelled after the dwelling-places of the living, and I think the "idea" of the "horned cairns" is taken from that of a cave-dwelling in a sinuously eaten-out limestone promontory, such as you may see many of in South Wales. It was, indeed, whilst working out the rubble filling up one of those caves, just as you worked out the rubble in the "West Tump," that I came to see the likeness. This likeness, I should add, anybody else may see who will compare your plans of the "West Tump" with a ground plan of one of these caverns. By saying, as I did for the first time in public, at the meeting of the British Association at Swansea, last autumn, that the "idea" of the horned cairn was to be found in a cave-containing headland, I mean that the one structure has been made after the pattern of the other; just as the "idea" of a Gothic cathedral is to be found in an avenue of trees; or the "idea" of a Saxon urn, with its equatorial angularity and Vandyked pattern, is to be found in the appearance which a holly-leaf presents when held by its stalk with the under surface towards the spectator. The bones from the "West Tump" are like all bones from similar barrows which have been through my hands, and in the following points :—They belonged to a short-statured but long-headed race of men, who were, if we may judge at all from what we see of living men of the same osteological character, darkish in complexion and hair. I have seen many such in this part of the world, being, as it is, a part of the world where pristine races are likely to survive, "the two voices, one of the sea, one of the mountains," favouring the chances which feebler folk have of escaping extirpation at the hands of stronger. But such men and such women may be found in many parts of even the most Saxonized and Danicized counties of England, and notably in Gloucestershire, which is such a county. I am perfectly certain that a sufficiently extensive set of bones from any real "horned cairn" would be distinguishable from any equally numerous and fairly selected, or similarly selected set of bones, from any other variety of interment in Great Britain, from those of the bronze period down to those of yesterday inclusive. Irrespective of any manganese or black fungus markings or discolorations, you will find peculiarities specified by me elsewhere (*e.g.* in "British Barrows," in my Paper on "The People of the Long Barrow Period," and on the tickets sent to Cheltenham with the "West Tump" skulls) in a collection of cranial and other bones from a Long Barrow, which you will either not find at all or find in very much smaller proportion per cent. in a collection from any other source. This statement, if true, is of great importance, both as regards the age of these interments and as regards the variability of our own species. I shall be glad to have the opportunity of showing its truth by a statistical examination of this particular set of Long Barrow bones when I return to England. Lastly, the broken state of many of the skeletons has been explained by some writers as being indicative of human sacrifices, &c. I think those persons who exposed themselves to constantly recurring avalanches of stones in the "West Tump" excavations, or *exsaxations*, will allow that these avalanches are a *vera ac sufficiens causa* for that broken state of the bones, and that the theory of successive interments which is absolutely necessary for explaining the *number* of the bodies, will also account for the commination which so many of them have suffered.

"With very kind regards, I am yours very truly,

"G. ROLLESTON."

"P.S.—Please have this printed with your Paper."

See "Proceedings Bristol and Glou. Archæ. Soc.," vol. v., p. 201.

No. 36.—WHITFIELD TUMP.

The remains of this long barrow are to be found on Minchinhampton Common, a little to the north of the Amberley Camp, and about two miles south of Stroud. It has been so much disturbed that it is difficult to ascertain its original form and dimensions. Its direction was east-south-east and west-north-west, the highest part being towards the east-south-east. Mr. Playne states the probable dimensions at seventy-five feet by thirty-six feet, but I think it must have been much longer than here stated in its original form.

See "Proceedings Cott. Nat. Field Club," vol. v., p. 279.

No. 37.—WILLERSEY BARROW.

There is a mound in Willersey Camp, on the top of the Cotteswold Hills, one and a half miles from Broadway, very much like a long barrow, though without excavation it would be impossible to be certain as to its nature. Its length is 160 feet, greatest width 66 feet, and greatest height four feet six inches. Its direction is east and west, the highest portion being at the east end. The interior seems to be composed of oolitic rubble and slabs, similar to that found in other Gloucestershire barrows.

No. 38.—WITHINGTON BARROW.

In the middle of Withington Wood, one mile south of the village and seven miles from Cheltenham, is a long barrow about 150 feet in length. Its direction is north-east and south-west, the highest portion lying towards the north-east. Several stones—forming chambers—are exposed, and it is evident that excavations have been made at some time and some of the chambers examined; but no record has been kept, and nothing is known as to what was found.

No. 39.—COLD ASTON LONG BARROW.

This is situated in the parish of Cold Aston or Aston Blank, one mile north-west of the village, and one and a half miles from Bourton-on-the-Water. Its length is 120 feet; greatest width 48 feet, and height about seven feet. Its direction is south-south-east and north-north-west, the highest portion being at the south-south-east end. A great number of flint arrow-heads have been found at various times in the immediate vicinity.

No. 40.—FARMINGTON LONG BARROW.

This lies inside the intrenchments of Norbury Camp, in the parish of Farmington, one mile north-east of Northleach. It is 200 feet in length, 100 feet wide, and five feet high, its direction being south-east and north-west. There is a large stone lying flat on the surface which may probably belong to one of the chambers. The barrow has never been examined.

END OF LONG BARROWS.

ROUND BARROWS.

The Round Barrows of Gloucestershire are very numerous, but so few of them have been examined that it is impossible to give an accurate account of many of them. I propose, therefore, firstly, to speak of those which have been described in other works, and then to give a list of many more hitherto unnoticed, without regard to their alphabetical order.

No. 1.—BOWNHILL.

This lies close to the long barrow above the village of Woodchester, three miles south-west of Stroud, and two miles north-west of Nailsworth. It was 60 feet in diameter, but has now been ploughed down.

See "Proceedings Cott. Nat. Field Club," vol. v., p 278.

No. 2.

This is in a field near the Windmill, on Minchinhampton Common, two miles south of Stroud. It was 60 feet in diameter, but has been nearly obliterated. The only articles found during the examination were an iron ring and a few fragments of bronze.

See "Proceedings Cott. Nat. Field Club," vol. v., p. 283.

No. 3.

This stands above the village of Hyde, three miles south-east of Stroud. It was 65 feet in diameter when examined, and only 30 inches in height, having been much levelled by the plough. In the centre of this was a circular excavation in the original soil, five feet in diameter and ten inches deep. The sides of this depression were protected by stones placed on edge. It was filled with burnt earth and contained fragments of burnt bones, some rude pottery, pebbles, a small piece of bronze, and a leaf-shaped arrow-head of flint.

See "Proceedings Cott. Nat. Field Club.," vol. v., p. 283.

No. 4.

In Gatcombe Wood, one mile south-east of Minchinhampton village. This is 35 feet in diameter and two feet high.

See "Proceedings Cott. Nat. Field Club," vol. v., p. 278.

No. 5.—THE OVEN.

This is situated in Avening Copse, half a mile west of the village of Avening, and one and a half miles south of Minchinhampton. It is 50 feet in diameter and five feet high. Charcoal and ashes were found scattered on the original surface, and in the centre of the mound a handful of burnt human bones and two worked flints were found.

See " Proceedings Cott. Nat. Field Club," vol. v., p. 281.

No. 6.

In Hazlewood, one mile south-east of Nailsworth. It is 75 feet in diameter, and three feet high.

See " Proceedings Cott. Nat. Field Club," vol. v., p. 278.

No. 7.

Near Hazlewood Copse, one mile south-east of Nailsworth. It was 67 feet in diameter, but is now ploughed down.

See "Proceedings Cott. Nat. Field Club," vol. v., p. 278.

No. 8.—LECHMORE.

This lies a few hundred yards south of the Lechmore long barrow, one and a half miles south of Nailsworth. It was 45 feet in diameter, and five feet high. The top of the mound consisted of stone and rubble 18 inches in depth, the bottom portion being fine mould. In this fine mould no less than 80 flints were discovered, 4 pieces of pottery ornamented with a pattern of dotted lines, and some teeth of oxen. Exactly in the centre of the barrow was a hole 8 inches deep, containing some burnt human bones.

See " Proceedings Cott. Nat. Field Club," vol. v., p. 278.

No. 9.

Near Chavenage Green, two and a half miles south-east of Nailsworth. It was about 60 feet in diameter, but is now ploughed down. The primary interment contained charcoal, burnt bones, small pieces of pottery, and a well-worked flint javelin point. In the secondary interment, discovered in 1847, were found iron spear-heads, bronze fibulæ, silver ear-rings, and stone, clay, and amber beads.

See "Journal Archæ. Assoc.," vol. iv., p. 50.
Also "Proceedings Cott. Nat. Field Club," vol. v., p. 282.

No. 10.

This is also near Chavenage Green, 100 yards distant from the last. It was 60 feet in diameter.

See "Journal of Archæological Association," vol. iv., p. 50.
Also " Proceedings Cott. Nat. Field Club," vol. v., p. 282.

No. 11.—Horsley Wood Tumulus.

This lies one mile from Horsley, and two miles south-west of Nailsworth. It was 52 feet in diameter, and three feet six inches high. A heap of ashes and burnt human bones were found in the centre on a level with the original surface; one piece of pottery and two teeth of an ox were also found.

See "Proceedings Cott. Nat. Field Club," vol. v., p. 284.

No. 12.—The Hyde Tumulus.

This lies three miles south-east of Stroud. Though not circular it has no connection with long barrows, and is therefore inserted here. It is 80 feet long, 60 feet wide, its height being 10 feet, and its direction east by north and west by south. This is probably of much later date than the other tumuli, either round or long; probably it was of Roman origin. It was opened in 1848, when a chamber was discovered enclosed by large stones. In this were found burnt bones and ashes, also a bronze fibula of Roman type.

See " Proceedings Cott. Nat. Field Club," vol. v., p. 284.

No. 13.—Dry Heathfield Tumulus.

Situated two miles south of Cheltenham. It was opened in 1860, and measured 60 feet in diameter. There was a chamber in the centre 6 feet long, 2 feet wide, and 2 feet deep, the sides and ends of which were formed of neat dry walling of Stonesfield slate. In this were found the remains of at least seven skeletons. The barrow had, however, been disturbed on some previous occasion.

See "Anthropological Review," vol. iii., p. 68.
Also " Proceedings Cott. Nat. Field Club," vol. vi., p. 334.

No. 14.—Foxcote Tumulus.

This lies on the top of the hill, one mile south of Dowdeswell, and four miles south-east of Cheltenham. It consists of loose stones, and measures from north to south 78 feet, and from east to west 69 feet, its height being eight feet. There was a dry wall built across the barrow, and near the centre was a chamber formed of flat stones placed on their edges and covered with stones two feet square; in this chamber were found the remains of one skeleton (a female). Fourteen flint flakes were also found with burnt stones, earth, and bones. Between 300 and 400 Roman coins were found in the black earth near the surface.

See "Anthropological Review," vol. iii., p. 69.
Also " Proceedings Cott. Nat. Field Club," vol. vi., p. 335.

Nos. 15, 16, and 17.

Three round barrows were opened many years ago on Cleeve Hill, beyond the racing stables, four miles north-east of Cheltenham. They all contained human bones.

See Rudder's "History of Gloucestershire," p. 369.
Also " Anthrop. Review," vol. iii., p. 70.

No. 18.

This lies half a mile south-west of Snowshill village and two and a half miles south of Broadway. It was examined in January, 1881. It is 66 feet in diameter and five feet six inches high, but previous to the examination it had been much reduced in height by the plough, and now has been obliterated. There was a chamber in the centre, four feet long, three feet wide, and two feet six inches high, formed of large slabs of stone; in this were found a number of human bones and several portions of a skull, much broken; also a bronze spear-head with socket, nine and a half inches long; a spear-head or dagger, eight and a half inches long; a bronze pin, six and a half inches in length; and a stone implement, six and a half inches long, with a cutting edge at one end and a hammer at the other; this is a beautifully worked implement, and has a hole through the centre for a handle.

Nos. 19 and 20.

There are two other round barrows in the same field as the last. Both have evidently been opened at some time, but unfortunately no record has been kept of their contents.

No. 21.

This lies three-quarters of a mile north of the last, two miles south of Broadway. It was opened many years ago, when bronze spear-heads and other articles were discovered, but I have been unable to get any information as to their character.

No. 22.

This lies in the parish of Cubberley, to the north of Cowley Manor, four miles south of Cheltenham. It consisted of a mound of earth and stones, no chamber being present. A skeleton was discovered in the centre in a sitting posture, and with it some flint flakes and round balls of sun-dried clay; the skull, which was sent to the Ethnological Society, appears to have been of the dolicho-cephalic type, similar to those found in long barrows. A flint from this barrow is in the Cheltenham College Museum.

See "Proceedings Cott. Nat. Field Club," vol. vi., p. 332.

No. 23.—THE CRIPPETTS' ROUND BARROW.

This lies a few hundred yards south of the Crippetts' Long Barrow, three miles south of Cheltenham.

Nos. 24, 25, AND 26.

These are three interesting barrows near the "Air Balloon," four miles south of Cheltenham. They lie in a coppice on the south side of the road leading from Cheltenham to Birdlip. One of these is about fourteen feet high, and has a circular depression in the centre; the others are very small, lying near to it.

No. 27.

In a field in the parish of Cranham, one and a half miles south-west of Birdlip, a barrow was opened by Mr. Dorington, and inspected by the County Archæological Society, in July, 1880. It has two walls forming a passage through the centre. Two skeletons were found imbedded in burnt masses of lime and stone; the burnt mass was eighteen inches in thickness, with the skeletons in the middle of it. Professor Rolleston pronounced this barrow one of the oldest forms of round tumuli, being a transition one between the long and round.

See "Transactions Bristol and Glou. Archæ. Soc.," vol. v., p. 133.

Nos. 28 AND 29.

Both these are situated near the above, between Hazel Hanger Wood and Foster's Ash, one and a half miles south-west of the village of Brimpsfield.

No. 30.

Within the intrenchment of Saintbury Camp, two miles north-west of Broadway. Diameter, forty feet; Height, four feet.

ROUND BARROWS.

No. 31.

On Scarborough Farm, in the parish of Cutsdean, half a mile to the east of Buggilde Street. Diameter, sixty feet; Height, five feet.

No. 32.

One mile east of the village of Temple Guiting, adjoining the ancient Buggilde Street. Diameter, sixty-five feet; Height, five feet.

Nos. 33, 34, 35, AND 36.

On Benborough Farm, in the parish of Temple Guiting, five miles north-west of Bourton-on-the-Water. Diameter of the first, sixty-six feet; Height, four feet six inches. Diameter of the second, fifty feet; Height, two feet. The remaining ones were removed a few years ago.

No. 37.—NOSE HILL BARROW.

By the side of Buggilde Street, one and a half miles north of the village of Naunton. Diameter, seventy-five feet; Height, four feet.

No. 38.

In Kineton Thorns, two miles north of Naunton. Diameter, thirty-three feet; Height, three feet.

Nos. 39, 40, 41, 42, 43, 44, 45, AND 46.

On Cow Common, in the parish of Lower Swell, two and a half miles from the village. These lie in the same field as Swell Long Barrow No. 1, and were examined by Canon Greenwell and Professor Rolleston.

See "British Barrows," p. 445, &c.

No. 47.—ALCOTS BARROW.

Half a mile south of the village of Condicote. (This name occurs in *Codex Diplomaticus*.) Diameter, ninety feet; Height, three feet six inches.

Nos. 48 AND 49.

These are twin barrows, known as Pegler's Knobb, one mile north-west of Upper Swell village, and two miles from Stow-on-the-Wold.

Nos. 50 AND 51.

These lie one mile north-west of Longborough and three and a half miles from Stow-on-the-Wold, near the Stow and Broadway Road. Diameter of the first, eighty feet; Height, nine feet.

No. 52.

Three-quarters of a mile south-west of Longborough, near the entrance gates of Banksfee House.

No. 53.

Close to Little Ganborough, two miles north-west of Stow-on-the-Wold.

No. 54.

Half a mile south-west of Donnington village, and one and a half miles from Stow-on-the-Wold.

No. 55.—PICKED MORDEN.

Two miles west of Lower Swell, and three miles from Stow-on-the-Wold. Diameter, eighty-six feet; Height, eight feet.

No. 56.

Half a mile west of Lower Swell.

No. 57.

A barrow was opened at Oddington, two miles east of Stow-on-the-Wold, in 1787. It was formed of layers of stones, and contained the bones of at least six skeletons, perforated beads of blue, red, and green, a fibula of copper, the centre of a shield, and spear-heads.

See Fosbrooke's " History of Gloucestershire," p. 406.
Also King's " Munimenta Antiqua," vol. i., p. 312.

ROUND BARROWS.

Nos. 58 AND 59.

On Hethel Farm, near the Foss Way, three-quarters of a mile south-west of Stow Station.

No. 60.—WAGBOROUGH.

On the side of Buggilde Street, in the parish of Upper Slaughter, one and a half miles north-west of Bourton-on-the-Water. Diameter, forty-eight feet; Height, six feet.

No. 61.—WYCK BEACON.

On the east of the road from Stow-on-the-Wold to Burford, one mile north-east of Little Rissington village.

No. 62.

On Bourton Hill Farm, one mile south of Bourton-on-the-Water.

No. 63.

On Clapton Hill, three-quarters of a mile north-east of Clapton village, and one and a half miles south of Bourton-on-the-Water.

Nos. 64, 65, AND 66.

These are three barrows on Leygore Farm, one mile south-east of Turkdean village, and one and a half miles north of Northleach.

No. 67.

Near Under Camp Farm, in the parish of Farmington, half a mile north-east of the village.

No. 68.

Just outside Norbury Camp, in the parish of Farmington, one mile north-east of Northleach.

No. 69.

On the west side of the Salt Way, three-quarters of a mile south-west of Salperton village, on a very high part of the Cotswold Hills, in the same field as Salperton Camp.

ROUND BARROWS.

No. 70.

On the farm known as Soundborough, three-quarters of a mile south of Sevenhampton, near the Banbury and Cheltenham Railway.

Nos. 71 AND 72.

Within the intrenchments of Oxenton Hill Camp, six miles north of Cheltenham.

No. 73.

At the top of Lineover Wood, three and a half miles south-east of Cheltenham.

No. 74.

On the top of Leckhampton Hill, on the east side of the principal fortification of the camp. It is very peculiar in form, the plan of it being nearly square, measuring thirty-five feet in each direction, and four feet high. It is defended by a mound two feet six inches high running all round it. Portions of human skeletons have lately been discovered in the centre.

No. 75.

Chedworth Beacon, between the villages of Chedworth and Colesbourne, one mile north-west of the former.

No. 76.

Half a mile north of the last, above Chedworth Woods, one mile south-west of the Chedworth Roman Villa.

No. 77.

On the high ground above Rendcomb Old Park, one mile south-west of the village of Rendcomb,

No. 78.

In Miserden Park, two and a quarter miles south of Brimpsfield village.

ROUND BARROWS. 105

No. 79.—JACK BARROW.

This stood on high ground between Duntisbourne Abbots and Edgeworth, but has been entirely removed, and a rickyard is now to be found on its site. The skeletons found were removed to Daglingworth Churchyard, and a stone erected over them to tell their history.

No. 80.

In the parish of Duntisbourne Abbots, near to the Duntisbourne Long Barrow. Diameter, thirty-five feet; Height, four feet.

No. 81.

Also in the parish of Duntisbourne Abbots, close to the last; now nearly obliterated by the plough.

No. 82.—MONEY TUMP.

In the parish of Bisley, three-quarters of a mile south of the village. Diameter, seventy feet; height, four feet six inches. Many worked flints have been found in its immediate neighbourhood.

Nos. 83 AND 84.

These lie between "Money Tump" and Lypiatt Park, a quarter of a mile west of the former.

No. 85.

On the top of the hill above Standish Park, three-quarters of a mile south-east of Haresfield Camp. Diameter, fifty feet; Height, eight feet.

No. 86.

Within 200 yards of the last named. Diameter, thirty feet; Height, eight feet.

No. 87.—HARESFIELD BEACON.

Within the intrenchments of Haresfield Camp, six miles south of Gloucester.

No. 88.

On the summit of Randwick Hill, two miles north-west of Stroud, 200 yards north-east of the Randwick Long Barrow, and within the intrenchments of Randwick Camp. Diameter, thirty-two feet ; Height, four feet.

No. 89.

This lies twenty-four feet south of the last. Diameter, twenty-seven feet ; Height, three feet.

No. 90.

On Symonds Hall Hill, two miles south-east of Dursley.

Nos. 91 AND 92.

On Symonds Hall Farm, two and a half miles south-east of Dursley.

No. 93.

In the parish of Lasborough, close to the village, four miles east of Wotton-under-Edge.

Nos. 94 AND 95.

On Wortley Hill, one mile east of Wotton-under-Edge.

No. 96.

One mile south-west of the village of Boxwell, and two and a half miles from Wotton-under-Edge.

Nos. 97 AND 98.

Near Knightsgrove, two miles south-west of the village of Leighterton.

No. 99.

One mile north of Oldbury-on-the-Hill.

No. 100.

Near Bowldown Wood, one and a half miles north-east of Leighterton village.

ROUND BARROWS.

No. 101.

Near the road from Bath to Stroud, one mile north-west of Oldbury-on-the-Hill.

Nos. 102, 103, AND 104.

Near the same road as the last, and lying due east of Oldbury-on-the-Hill.

No. 105.

Near Crickstone Farm, one and a quarter miles north-west of Badmington, and the same distance north-east of Sodbury Camp.

Nos. 106, 107, AND 108.

One mile south-east of Tormarton, on the borders of Gloucestershire and Wiltshire.

No. 109.

One mile south of Tormarton and close to Hebdown Camp.

No. 110.

On Marshfield Down, one mile north-east of Marshfield.

Nos. 111 AND 112.

In Wiltshire, one and a half miles east of Badmington, near Alderton.

No. 113.

One and a half miles south of Alderley.

No. 114.

Near North Stoke, two miles east of Bitton.

No. 115.

Close to the village of Bitton, a little to the west of the Camp.

No. 116.

In Over Park, one and a half miles south-west of Almondsbury, and one mile from Knole Park Camp.

Nos. 117 and 118.

Near the Ship Inn, one mile and a quarter south of Thornbury.

No. 119.

On Tidenham Chase, one and a half miles north-east of Chepstow.

No. 120.

One mile from Blakeney and two miles south of Newnham.

No. 121.—Waste Tumulus.

Near Brockhampton, five miles east of Cheltenham. It was sixty feet in diameter. Near the centre was a chamber formed by flat stones and dry walling, eighteen inches deep, eight feet long, and two feet wide. It contained seven skeletons, and was covered over with rough stones, in the form of a roof. Several flint flakes were found during the excavations.

See "Anthrop. Review," vol. iii., p. 69.

Nos. 122, 123, 124, 125, and 126.

The remains of four other tumuli were discovered in the same field as the last, and another about 100 yards to the south, apparently undisturbed.

See "Anthrop. Review," vol. iii., p. 69.

END OF ROUND BARROWS.

BRITISH AND ROMAN ROADS.

AKEMAN STREET,

Or Akman Street, seems to have been a name given to that portion of the Foss Way which runs from Cirencester to Bath. It has been seriously described by some writers as an Anglo-Saxon name, signifying the Sick Man's Road, referring to the principal highway to the celebrated hot baths of Aquæ Sulis (Bath). Jackment's Bottom, the point at which the Ikenild Street leaves the Foss Way, four miles south-west of Cirencester, probably has the same derivation as Akman.

BUGGILDE STREET.

This ancient road runs from the Ryknield Street, near Bidford, in Warwickshire, and proceeds by Honeybourne and Weston-sub-Edge, ascending the Cotswold Hills near Saintbury and Willersey Camps; then, leaving Broadway Tower on the west, it runs along the ridge of the hills above Snowshill, with its round barrows, above Upper and Lower Guiting, with barrows on each side of it; then on by Wagborough, and joins the Foss Way near Bourton-on-the-Water. At its junction with the Foss there is a fine Roman Villa. (See Bourton Villa.) The first mention of this road known to me is in a Saxon Charter, printed in Kemble's *Codex Diplomaticus*, No. 61, dated 709, in which certain boundaries are described as "running along Bugghilde Streete, on Stanihtan Hyll." In another Charter, dated 967, it is called "Bucgan Streete." At Weston-sub-Edge it is still known as "Buckle Street." It passes near the village of Buckland, also by Brockhill and

Buggyhill, now called Beckyhill. The road is raised in several places near Kineton Thorns, and where so raised it has a uniform width of nearly eight feet.

See " Transactions Bristol and Glou. Archæ. Soc.," vol. iv., p. 213.

CONDICOTE LANE.

This is a perfectly straight portion of a Roman Road, leading from Condicote Camp to the Cheltenham and Stow Road (called in an old charter the " Via Regia "). In several places the road is raised three feet above the adjoining lands, and where so raised has a uniform width of about thirteen feet. Probably this road extended further in each direction; towards the north it ran by Hinchwick Camp, and towards the south to Salmonsbury Camp, at Bourton-on-the-Water. A glance at the map will show that its direction is pointing directly to the latter place, though little or no trace of its course can now be found.

CRIBB'S CAUSEWAY.

This is a local name for a portion of the Western Trackway which ran from Carlisle to Exeter. Cribb's Causeway seems to have commenced at Almondsbury. Leaving that portion of the Western Trackway called the Ridgeway, it proceeds by Knole Park Camp to Henbury, thence by Blaize Castle and King's Weston Camp to Abone, crossing the river Avon into Somersetshire near Sea Mills.

ERMINE STREET.

Most antiquaries are agreed in opinion that this was originally a British Trackway. Its name is thought to be derived from Ερμης (Mercurius), who is said to have presided over the highways. The road runs from Spinæ, now called Speen, near Newbury, probably to Abergavenny and St. David's. It enters Gloucestershire about three miles north-west of Cricklade, through which place it passes. It then runs between

Siddington and Preston to Corinium, now Cirencester ; thence by Stratton, leaving the Bagendon Earthworks and Combend Villa to the east, and, passing near the villages of Elkstone and Brimpsfield, it reaches Birdlip. Here it is protected on the south side by a strong mound, and many Roman coins and other antiquities have been found when excavating for the foundation of houses near its course. After leaving Birdlip it descended the escarpment of the Cotswold Hills, but not on the line of the present road. It turned sharply to the west into Witcomb Wood, through the present lodge gates, and after pursuing its westerly course for nearly a quarter of a mile it turned round to the north, its old course being still visible, descending the hill by a far better gradient than the present road, and sunk several feet below the surface. It crossed the line of the present road near the sixth milestone from Gloucester, and rejoined it at the bottom of the hill. Leaving Witcomb Villa and the great camp on Cooper's Hill to the left, it pursued its course direct to Wotton, and thence, turning to the west, it entered Glevum (Gloucester). In lowering the road at the point where the Bristol and Birmingham Railway crosses it, the Roman pavement was discovered eighteen inches below the present level ; the pavement was so well constructed that the engineers had to resort to blasting operations to assist in its removal. Entering Gloucester by the North Gate, and leaving it by the West Gate, it crosses the river Severn and Alney Island, and, passing Highnam, it leaves Huntly to the north and Longhope to the South, finally leaving Gloucestershire three-quarters of a mile east of Mitcheldean Road Station, on the Hereford and Gloucester Railway ; thence it runs to Ross, Abergavenny, and probably to St. David's.

Forest of Dean Roman Roads.

These are so numerous that it will be impossible in this work to describe them all. In that invaluable little guide called " A Week's Holiday in the Forest of Dean," published by Mr. John Bellows, of Gloucester, it is stated that nearly every road in the Forest of Dean is a Roman Way, and that the precise date at which these Forest of Dean Roads were made cannot be fixed, but that we have clear evidence that it was considerably earlier than the close of the 1st century. A portion of the Via Julia, running a little to the west of Welshbury and Little Dean Camps at Tibb's Cross, with the original Roman pavement still preserved, was examined a few years back by the members of the Cotteswold Field Club. In describing the continuation of this road near Blackpool Bridge, the guide above referred to says that a good deal of the paving is still visible, it being perfect for 100 yards up to Blackpool Bridge. The bifurcation made by the Roman engineers is distincily traceable, by which, while the main road went straight on through the brook, a branch of it passed over the bridge to enable the traffic to be carried on in flood time. The pavement is seven feet ten and a half inches in width, and consists of cubes of conglomerate or millstone grit eight or ten inches square, with margins or kerbstones five inches wide and from ten to twenty inches in length. In many parts of the Forest of Dean the same kind of pavement is visible. Any one walking from the Speech House Railway Station to the Speech House will notice it in several places. The reason, no doubt, for there being so many Roman roads in the Forest must be attributed to the extensive mines worked by the Romans in this district, and in the position it occupies, with Glevum (Gloucester) on the north-east, Blestium (Monmouth) on the west, and Lydney and Caerwent on the south. In some places the margin stones which keep the central cubes in their position are in their turn supported by a line of heavy blocks firmly bedded in the ground in such a way as to bear against the points of the kerbstones. An excellent example of this exists on the road from Little Dean to Newnham, opposite the New Zealand Inn. The principal highway which passes by the Forest of Dean, and which I call the Gloucester branch of the Via Julia is further described under the head of "Via Julia." The next in importance, a portion of which has been described in detail, comes from the north, by Mitcheldean, Welshbury Camp, Littledean Camp, Blackpool Bridge, and probably Lydney, with its fine Camps and Villa. Another important road leads through the Forest from Littledean, by Cinderford Station to Coleford and Monmouth. Another runs from Mitcheldean, by Drybrook, to Coleford. There are others leaving the Via Julia—one at Westbury-on-Severn, by Flaxley ; another from Newnham to Littledean, and there are two lines of Roman Roads from Littledean to Mitcheldean. The above are the most important Roman Roads in the district ; but, as I before mentioned, nearly every highway in the Forest of Dean was originally Roman, and, possibly, many of them British.

Foss Way.

This well-known road has been the subject of much difference of opinion among antiquaries as to its origin. For instance, the Rev. T. Leman says, "It was a British Road, running from the north-eastern coast of Lincolnshire, through several important British towns, to the great British port of Seaton, in Devonshire ;" while Dr. Guest states, "The name Foss has given rise to some strange hypotheses ; it has been supposed that the road was so called because it was one of the hollow ways which marked out the lines of ancient British traffic ; but, in truth, the Roman character of the Foss is perhaps more decided than that of any other highway in the kingdom." I cannot help thinking that there was a British trackway on the line of the Foss, long, long before the days of Cæsar, though no doubt the Romans improved it ; but I will not stop to discuss that point now. The Foss Way seems to have started from Portus Felix, at the mouth of the Humber, passing Lindum (Lincoln), Ratæ (Leicester), Benonis (Claychester), Corinium (Cirencester), Aquæ Sulis (Bath), Ischalis (Ilchester), terminating at the port of Moridunum (Seaton), on the coast of Devonshire. It enters Gloucestershire at Dorn, near to Moreton-in-the-Marsh, passing close to Batsford Camp, and through the town of Moreton; it ascends the hills to Stow-on-the-Wold, leaving Swell Villa to the west, and descends to Bourton Bridge, where it is joined by Buggilde Street. Here there are many Roman buildings contiguous to its course, and the fine Camp of Salmonsbury is only half a mile distant. Regardless of steep hills, it now pursues its way to Cirencester, passing close to Norbury Camp at Farmington, and within half a mile of Northleach. It crosses the Salt Way near Stowell Park, and joins the Ikenild Street one mile to the north-west of Cirencester. Leaving this, it continues its course to Bath, leaving the county near Trewsbury Camp; but for several miles it forms the county boundary. In many places it is raised a considerable height above the adjoining district, with a deep ditch on each side. On its course from Cirencester to Bath it passes the Roman Station of Whitewalls.

Green Street.

This has been described as a Roman Road, running round the southern side of Churchdown Hill, crossing the Ermine Street near Brockworth, and joining the Sarn Way near the foot of Cooper's Hill, at a small hamlet still called Green Street.

Green Way.

There are two ancient roads called the Green Way in Gloucestershire, one running by Badgworth and Shurdington, and ascending the steep escarpment of the Cotswold Hills, the other leading from Norbury Camp, at Farmington, by Puesdown and Shipton Olive to the great Roman Station at Wycomb, near Andoversford, and continuing its course, probably, along the hills to Cleeve Hill and Nottingham Hill Camps.

Ikenild Street.

This is so called from the Iccĕni or Ikkens. It runs from the eastern side of the Island, and passes Kirklington, Woodstock, and Stonefield, crossing the river Evenlode to Wilcote, and so to Ramsden, a little beyond which village it can be traced at Whitty Green ; but from this point, by Astally, and so through the fields to Bradwell Grove, it is scarcely visible. Nevertheless, there it is again to be seen holding a straight course into Gloucestershire, passing by Coln St. Aldwyn to Corinium (Cirencester), and joining the Foss Way one mile before reaching that town. After leaving Cirencester it runs on the same line as the Foss as far as Jackments Bottom, passing near Trewsbury Camp. It then branches off to Rodmarton and Cherrington, at both of which places there are Roman Villas. " It then traverses the turnpike from Tetbury to Hampden, passes a house called the Star and Garter to Chavenage Green, from whence it is an obscure horse-way through the fields to the Bath Road (which it crosses about a quarter of a mile before the separation of the Rodborough and Frocester Roads). It then descends into Lasborough Vale with a kind of sweep, and winds up the opposite hill to regain its course, having, as usual, tumuli for a direction on each side. It passes the inclosures by the edge of the valley in which Bagpath Village is placed, tending towards a vast tumulus on the brow of the hill, close to the road leading to Dursley and Rodborough." It then runs along Symond's Hall Hill to the ridge above Wotton-under-Edge, where it descends the hill and all trace of it is lost. It probably continued by Elbury Hill to Cromhall, where there is a Roman Villa, and thence by Tytherington and Abbey Camps to Elberton, with its ancient camp, and Aust, where it crossed the river Severn, and joined the Via Julia, near Venta Silurum (Caerwent).

OAKLE STREET.

A short road, only a mile and a half in length, forming a junction between the Ermine Street and the Gloucester branch of the Via Julia, four and a half miles west of Gloucester.

Patch Way.

This appears to be a local name of probably a Roman road leaving the ancient Western Trackway at Almondsbury, at the point where Cribbs Causeway and the Ridgeway join, and proceeding nearly due south by Patchway Green to Filton, and thence by Horfield to Bristol, crossing the main line of the Via Julia before arriving at that town.

Port Way.

This leaves Gloucester by the Eastgate, and proceeds in a south-easterly direction by Matson and Upton St. Leonards, where a branch road leaves the main line and ascends the Cotswold Hills by Prinknash Park. The main road goes by Kimsbury Castle to Painswick, and then, probably, by Stroud, Woodchester Villa, Nailsworth, crossing the Ikenild Street near Calcot Farm, and then runs nearly south, attended by a large number of tumuli, by the great Roman camp at Sodbury, the Roman station at Cross Hands, leaving Tormarton to the east and Dyrham Camp half a mile to the west. It probably ran by Cold Ashton, Swainswick, and Little Salisbury Camps, and joined the Foss Way one mile north-east of Bath.

Ridgeway.

This is a local name given to that portion of the Western Trackway which runs from the Ship Inn, about one mile and a half south of Thornbury, to Almondsbury Hill, where it joins Cribbs Causeway and the Patch Way.

Ryknield Street.

This was a British Road, stated to commence at the mouth of the Tyne, and, passing the Watling Street at Catterick, it proceeded thence by Aldborough, crossing the Watling Street at Wall, thence through Sutton Coldfield to Birmingham, King's Norton, Alcester, Bidford, Sedgebarrow, Tewkesbury Berry Hill, near Ross, and probably by Abergavenny to St.

David's. This road is very difficult to trace through Gloucestershire, except from Sedgebarrow to Tewkesbury. It entered Gloucestershire somewhere between Childs Wickham and Evesham, and, running by Sedgebarrow and Beckford Inn, it probably crossed the river Severn at Tewkesbury; but whether it continued its course to Ross by Newent, or ran down the western side of the Severn to the Ermine Street, near Gloucester, I am at present unable to say.

Salt Way.

This is an old British trackway, which runs from Droitwich through Worcestershire, under the name of the Salt Way or the Salters Way. It enters Gloucestershire near Ashton-under-Hill, and probably ran by Dumbleton and Toddington to Hayles, though no trace of it can now be found. In Isaac Taylor's Map of Gloucestershire, dated 1800, the Salt Way is shown running through the villages above mentioned. There is also a barn standing on the line of this road near Elmley Castle called the "Salt Way Barn," and there is a field between Dumbleton and Toddington called "Salters Close." Near Hayles Abbey the road is distinctly to be traced in its ascent of the Cotswold Hills, and runs, attended in its course by tumuli, past Hawling, Salperton, and Hazleton, crossing the Foss Way between Northleach and Stowell Park; thence it proceeds by Crickley Barrow to Coln St. Aldwyns, where it crosses the Ikenild Street, and eventually leaves Gloucestershire at Lechlade on its way to the coast of Hampshire. It is mentioned in a Saxon Charter, dated 969, as "Sealt Street." Some have supposed the name to have arisen from the traffic of salt from Droitwich, while others hold that the name simply implies the "Hill Way."

Sarn Way.

This road ran from the Green Street at the bottom of Cooper's Hill through a portion of Witcomb Wood (a branch of it probably leading to the Witcomb Roman Villa in

"Sarundells"), joining the Ermine Street close to Birdlip. The pavement of this road can still be traced in places.

Via Julia.

The course of this road has been the subject of considerable discussion among antiquaries; but I think the following may be looked upon as the most probable solution of the difficulty. The main line of the road started from Isca Silurum (Caerleon), the head-quarters of the second legion of the Roman army, and passing Venta Silurum (Caerwent), Aqua Sulis (Bath), continued by Cunetio, near Marlborough, to Calever Atrebatum (Silchester), which seems to have been the great military centre of the south of Britain. This main line had, however, an important branch leaving it at, or near Caerwent, and running by Chepstow and Lydney to Gloucester. The stations on the main line are thus stated in the Itinerary of Antonine. Ab Isca :—Venta Silurum, M.P. VIIII.; Abone, M.P. VIIII.; Trajectus, VIIII.; Aquis Solis, M.P. VI. Bishop Clifford, in a paper read before the Somersetshire Archæological Society in 1876, after repeating the idea that the Via Julia crossed the river Severn to Aust, states that the road ran from Caerleon to Caerwent, and thence to Sudbrook Camp on the banks of the Severn, crossing the river at that point to Abone, near Henbury, and Blaize Castle, in Gloucestershire; thence it continued its course to Trajectus at Bitton, and on to Bath by the high ground passing the Lansdown Camps. After leaving Bath, its course can be easily traced onwards to Silchester. By adopting this course, the distances given in the Itinerary of Antonine are found to be correct. All other suppositions as to its route commence by stating that the distances as given in the Itinerary are wrong; but there seems no reason to doubt the accuracy of the figures, with such a clear proof before us that they might be quite correct. The branch of the Via Julia leading from Caerwent to Gloucester is not mentioned in any Itinerary; but as it has been traced the whole distance, the only difference of opinion can be whether it is correctly called part of the Via Julia. Leaving Caerwent by the east gate, it ran by the village of Crick towards Chepstow ; here it made a considerable detour in order to cross the river Wye. The ancient track can still be traced descending the wooded banks of that river some distance north of Chepstow, near Piercefield Park. It then ran by Combesbury Camp to Tidenham, and thence by Woolaston and Alveston to Lydney. (See under Lydney for Camps and Villas.) Leaving Lydney it took an inland direction by Soudley and Littledean Camps, thence bending to the east to Westbury-on-Severn. It then probably followed the line of the present road by Stantway and Minsterworth to Gloucester, forming a junction with the Ermine Street near Highnam Court, two and a half miles west of the city. Some details of this road are given under " The Forest of Dean Roman Roads." It is paved for a considerable distance, having an average width of eight Roman feet.

Western Trackway.

This British trackway must have been one of the most important ancient roads in England, and one that has been much overlooked by antiquaries. It seems to have originated at Luguballium (Carlisle), and ran by Coccium (Blackrode, Lancashire), Salinæ (Droitwich), Branogena (Worcester), thence by Tewkesbury to Gloucester (Glevum), though opinions differ as to which side of the river Severn the original road took between the last two towns. From Gloucester it pursued its southern course in a line nearly parallel with the present high road to Bristol, as far as Almondsbury, passing Hardwicke, Whitminster Inn, Stone, Abbey Camp, &c. After passing Almondsbury, it pursued the road now called " Cribbs Causeway," by Knole Park Camp, Blaize Castle, and King's Weston Camp, crossing the river Avon near Sea Mills, and thence pursuing its course by Uxella, near Bridgewater, and so on to Isca (Exeter), thus forming a direct road from the North of England to Devonshire.

White Way.

This was without doubt a Roman Road, running due north from Corinium (Cirencester) by Baunton Downs, North Cerney Downs, and Chedworth Beacon to the celebrated Roman Villa at Chedworth, and probably to the Withington Roman Villa, and so on along the Withington Road to the Dowdeswell Camps, and the great Roman Station at Wycomb, &c., thus giving access to many important Roman Stations and Villas from the great centre, Corinium.

There are, doubtless, many other British and Roman Roads in the county, such as "The Jack Way," "Pig Street," "The Calf Way," near Bisley, "Chittening Street," "Letch Lane," near Bourton-on-the-Water; the "Port Way," near Upper Slaughter; the road from the Cross Hands, by Chipping Sodbury and Iron Acton; the road near Thornbury, leading from the Western Trackway to Oldbury; the road running from the Via Julia, north-east of Chepstow and Beachley; and others, which may have been of British or Roman origin, such as the Via Regia, running by Wycomb, Lower Swell, and Stow-on-the-Wold; the road from Minchinhampton to Cirencester; and, doubtless, a communication existed between the numerous Camps on the escarpment of the Cotswold Hills, say from Leckhampton Hill Camp, by Crickley Hill Camp, Birdlip Camp, Cooper's Hill Camp, Kimsbury Camp, along Sponebed Hill to Haresfield Camp; and, lastly, the road from Gloucester, by Newent and Dymock, and so on to the north.

FINIS.

APPENDIX.

No. 113.—TYTHERINGTON CAMP.

This lies in the parish of Tytherington, two and a half miles south-east of Thornbury. It is very irregular in shape, for the greater part conforming to the natural outline of the hill. In those places where the escarpment does not form a sufficient defence it has a single mound and ditch. Rudder says, "This is generally supposed, from the construction and other circumstances, to be the work of the Romans, who had certainly a lodgment here, as may be concluded from a tessellated pavement dug up at Stidcot, in this parish." It seems, however, probable that it was of British origin.

See " Proceedings Cott. Nat. Field Club," vol. vi., p. 230.
Also " Rudder's History of Gloucestershire," p. 766.

ERRATA.

Page 10, line 9, for " Peninsular " read " Peninsula."
Page 50, line 6, after " this " insert " is."
Page 64, fourth line from foot, for " dixeunt " read " dixerunt."
Page 76, line 16, for " Champ " read " Camp."
Page 76, eleventh line from foot, for " Newmarsh " read " Newmarch."
Page 82, second line from foot, for " Nymphsfield " read " Nympsfield."
Page 83, lines 3 and 5, for " Nymphsfield " read " Nympsfield."
Page 88, ninth line from bottom, for " Hetty Pegley's Tump " read " Hetty Pegler's Tump."
Page 93, line 10, for " commination " read " comminution."
Page 107, line 4, for " east " read " west."

INDEX.

A

Abbey Camp, 1, 115, 119.
Abbey Lane, 1.
Abergavenny, 110, 111, 116.
Ablington Camp, 1.
Ablington Barrow, 73.
Abone, 2, 7, 29, 49, 110, 118.
Abston, 18.
Akeman Street, 109, 50.
Alcester, 116.
Alcots Barrow, 101.
Aldborough, 116.
Alderley, 107.
Alderton, 107.
Aldsworth, 30.
Almondsbury, 30, 107, 110, 116, 119.
Alney Island, 111.
Alveston, 1, 119.
Amberley, 3.
Amberley Camp, 2, 93.
Ampney Parish, 42.
Andoversford, 69, 114.
Antonines Itinerary, 2, 6, 49, 118.
Aqua Sulis, 6, 109, 113, 118.
Arlingham, 2.
Ashton-under-Hill, 117.
Astally, 115.
Avening, 25, 73, 88, 96.
Avening Barrow, 73.
Avon, 2, 14, 47, 49, 110, 119.
Avonmouth, 2.
Aubrey John, 81.
Aust, 115, 118.

B

Badgworth, 114.
Badmington, 107.
Bagendon, 3, 4, 111.
Bagpath, 115.
Baker, Mr., 12, 19, 27, 29, 55.
Bambury Stone, 8.
Banbury and Cheltenham Railway, 82, 104.
Banksfee, 102.
Barton Villa, 60.
Bath, 6, 19, 30, 46, 49, 53, 107, 109, 113, 114, 116, 118.
Bathurst, Lord, 77.
Bathurst, Hon. C., 63, 64.
Batsford Camp, 4.
Baunton, 120.
Beachley, 4, 39, 120.
Bearse Common, 47.
Beckbury, 4.
Beckets Bury, 6.

Beckford, 9, 117.
Belas Knapp, 74.
Bell, Captain, 60.
Bellows, Mr., 22, 112.
Benborough, 101.
Benonis, 113.
Berkeley, 7, 17.
Bibury 1, 30, 55.
Bibury Villa, 55.
Bidford, 109, 116.
Bigland, Mr., 38.
Bigswear, 5.
Birdlip, 5, 15, 16, 17, 89, 100, 111, 118, 120.
Birmingham, 116.
Bisley, 76, 78.
Bisley Barrow, 75.
Bisley Villa, 55.
Bitton, 6, 18, 22, 49, 50, 107, 118.
Bitton Camp, 6.
Blackenbury, 6.
Blackpool Bridge, 112, 113.
Blackrode, 119.
Blaize Castle, 7, 2, 27, 29, 110, 118, 119.
Blakeney, 108.
Blandford, 44.
Blestium, 112.
Blisbury, 7.
Bloody Acre Camp, 7.
Bos Pen, 45.
Bourton-on-the-Water, 14, 28, 36, 37, 43, 56, 94, 103, 109, 110, 114, 120.
Bourton Villa, 56, 109.
Bourton Hill Farm, 103.
Bowldown Wood, 106.
Bownhill Barrow, 75, 95.
Box, 36.
Boxwell, 81, 106.
Boyd River, 18.
Bradwell Grove, 115.
Branogena, 119.
Brayley, Mr., 28.
Bredon Camp, 8, 9.
Bredon Hill, 1, 8, 9, 24.
Briavel's, St., 5, 39, 47.
Bridgewater, 119.
Brimpsfield, 89, 100, 104, 111.
Bristol, 1, 2, 7, 13, 20, 29, 30, 40, 116, 119.
Britton, Mr., 28.
Broadway, 43, 52, 93, 99, 100, 102, 109.
Brockhampton, 108.
Brockhill, 109.
Brockworth, 114.
Brodbro' Green, 23, 62.
Brooke, Mr., 67.
Brookthorpe, 54.
Brownshill Villa, 56.
Buckholt, 16.

Buckland, 109.
Buckle Street, 109.
Buckman, Mr., 32, 60, 76.
Buggilde Street, 109, 101, 103 114.
Buggy Hill, 110.
Burford, 28, 103.
Bury Camp, 9.
Bury Hill Camp, 9.

C

Caer Bladon, 48.
Caer Cori, 16.
Caer Glou, 22.
Caerleon, 118.
Caer Oder, 14.
Caerwent, 2, 112, 115, 118, 119.
Caerwood Camp, 10.
Calcot Farm, 116.
Caleva, 118.
Calf Way, 120.
Cam, 10.
Cam Long Down, 10.
Camden, 19.
Camp Barrows, 76.
Carlisle, 110, 119.
Castle Coombe, 53.
Castle Godwin, 28.
Caswell Wood, 39.
Catterick, 116.
Ceawlin, King, 20.
Charlton Abbots Camp, 11, 74.
Charles, King, 29.
Chastleton Camp, 11.
Chedworth, 57, 104.
Chedworth Villa, 57, 56, 104, 120.
Chedworth Beacon, 104.
Cheltenham, 5, 9, 12, 17, 18, 24, 26, 31, 38, 40, 41, 46, 53, 60, 67, 69, 70, 74, 77, 94, 98, 99, 100, 104, 108, 110.
Chepstow, 1, 4, 10, 14, 54, 108, 118, 119, 120.
Cherrington Villa, 58.
Cherry Wood, 79.
Childs Wickham, 117.
Chittening Street, 120.
Churchdown, 11, 24, 114.
Cirencester, 1, 3, 16, 21, 36, 38, 40, 42, 50, 55, 57, 58, 61, 64, 67, 76, 77, 109, 111, 113, 114, 115, 120.
Cirencester Barrow, 76.
Clapton, 103.
Clarke, Mr., 20, 24.
Claychester, 113.
Cleeve, 12, 13.
Cleeve Hill Camp, 12, 13, 24, 26, 114.
Clifford, Bishop, 2, 6, 49, 118.
Clifton, 13.
Clifton Camp, 13, 27, 47.
Coates, 50.
Coccium, 119.
Cold Ashton, 116.
Cold Aston, 14.
Cold Aston Barrow, 94.
Cold Aston Camp, 14.
Coleford, 20, 47.
Colerne, 9.
Colesbourne, 37, 58, 104.
Coln River, 1, 67.
Coln St. Aldwyn, 115, 117.
Combend Villa, 58.
Combesbury Camp, 14.

Conderton, 9.
Condicote, 15, 21, 27, 101.
Condicote Camp, 15, 110.
Condicote Lane, 110.
Coombe Hill, 29.
Cooper's Hill Camp, 15, 66, 111, 114, 117, 120.
Corinium, 16, 60, 32, 38, 50, 62, 113, 115, 120.
Cow Common, 86, 101.
Cowley, 5, 99.
Cranham, 15, 100.
Cribbs Causeway, 110, 116, 119.
Crick, 119.
Cricklade, 110.
Crickley Barrows, 77.
Crickley Hill Camp, 17, 24, 60, 77, 120.
Crippetts Barrow, 77, 100.
Cromhall Villa, 59, 115.
Cross Hands, 116.
Cunetio, 118.
Cutham Lane, 3.
Cutsdean, 101.

D

Daglingworth Church, 105.
Daglingworth Villa, 61.
Damery Camp, 17.
Daniels Brook, 62.
Dee River, 39.
Denhel Hill Wood, 39.
Dent, Mrs., 66, 71.
Deorham, Battle of, 20.
Dodington Villa, 61, 62.
Donington, 102.
Dorington, Mr., 100.
Dorn, 4, 114.
Doverow Hill, 42.
Dowdeswell, 18, 98.
Dowdeswell Camps, 18, 120.
Doynton Camps, 18.
Drakestone, 19, 27.
Driver, Mr., 55.
Droitwich, 117, 119.
Drybrook, 113.
Dry Heathfield Tumulus, 98.
Dry Hill Villa, 60
Ducie, Earl of, 59.
Dumbleton, 117.
Duntisbourne Barrow, 77, 105.
Dursley, 6, 10, 19, 63, 65, 83, 88, 106, 115.
Dyrham Camp, 19, 116.

E

Eastington, 42.
Edgworth, 105.
Edgworth Barrow, 78.
Edward IV., King, 46.
Elberton, 20, 115.
Elberton Camp, 20.
Elbury, 115.
Eldon, Earl of, 57.
Elkstone, 111.
Elmley Castle, 117.
English Bicknor, 20.
Ermine Street, 110, 16, 42, 61, 67, 114, 115, 117, 118, 119.
Eubury Camp, 21, 15.
Evenlode, 28, 115.

Exeter, 110, 119.
Eyford Barrow, 78, 83.

F

Farmcote, 4
Farmington, 37, 103, 114.
Farmington Villa, 37.
Farmington Barrow, 94.
Farrer, Mr., 57.
Filton, 116.
Flaxley, 52, 113.
Fleming, Mr., 24.
Forest of Dean Roads, 111.
Fosbrooke, Mr., 48.
Foss Bridge, 57.
Foss Way, 113, 4, 7, 16, 37, 44, 45, 50, 53, 56, 109, 103, 115, 116, 117.
Foster's Ash, 100.
Foxcote Tumulus, 98.
Frampton Mansel Camp, 21.
Freezing Hill, 22.
Frocester, 115.

G

Ganborough, Little, 102.
Gatcombe Park, 88.
Gatcombe Wood, 96.
Ghyst, 13.
Giant's Stone Barrow, 79,
Glevum, 22, 15, 23, 62.
Gloucester, 1, 9, 11, 15, 22, 23, 24, 26, 28, 29, 54, 57, 62, 67, 77, 81, 105, 111, 112, 115, 117, 118, 119, 120.
Gomonde, Mr., 60.
Granville Monument, 31.
Green Street, 114.
Green Way, 114, 37.
Greenwell, Canon, 101.
Guest Dr., 113.
Guiting, 109.

H

Hayles Wood, 4, 117.
Hampden, 115.
Hardwicke, 119.
Haresfield Camp, 23, 1, 54, 62, 105, 120.
Haresfield Moat, 24, 33.
Haresfield Villa, 62.
Husleton Barrow, 79, 80, 117.
Hawling, 11, 117.
Hazel Hanger Wood, 100.
Hazel Wood, 96.
Hazel Wood Coppice Camp, 25.
Hazleton, 79, 80, 117.
Hebdown Camp, 25, 34, 107.
Hempstead Camp, 26.
Henbury, 7, 29, 110, 118.
Hethel Farm, 103.
Hetty Pegler's Tump, 88.
Hewlett's Camp, 26.
Highnam, 111, 119.
Hinchwiek Camp, 27, 110.
Hinton Hill, 19.
Hoar Stone Tumulus, 80.
Hod Hill, 44.
Honeybourne, 109.
Horfield, 116.
Horsley Wood Tumulus, 97.

Horton Camp, 27.
Hucclecote, 12.
Huddinknoll Hill, 54.
Humber, 113.
Humble Bee How, 74.
Huntley, 111.
Huntley, Matthew, 81.
Hyde, 95.
Hyde, Tumulus, 97.

I

Icomb Camp, 27.
Idbury Camp, 28.
Idols Barrow, 80.
Ikenild Street, 114, 16, 30, 42, 109, 116, 117.
Ilchester, 113.
Iron Acton, 120.
Isca Silurum, 118, 119.
Ischalis, 113.

J

Jack Barrow, 105.
Jackments Bottom, 109, 115.
Jack Way, 120.
Jones, Mr. J., 45.

K

Kemerton, 8.
Kimsbury, 28, 54, 120.
Kineton Thorns, 101, 110.
King, Mr., 46.
Kingscote Villa, 63.
Kingsholm, 23.
King's Norton, 116.
King Stanley, 45.
King's Weston, 29, 2, 7, 27, 110, 119.
Kirklington, 114.
Knights Grove, 106.
Knole Park Camp, 30, 107, 110, 119.

L

Ladborough Camp, 30.
Lansdown Camp, 30, 81, 118.
Lark's Bush, 21.
Lasborough, 106, 115.
Lawrence, Mrs., 70.
Leach River, 30.
Lechlade, 117.
Lechmore Barrow, 81, 96.
Leckhampton Camp, 81, 24, 104, 120.
Leckhampton Moat, 32, 24, 25.
Leicester, 113.
Leighterton, 106.
Leighterton Barrow, 81.
Leland, 49.
Leman, Rev. T., 13, 113.
Letch Lane, 37, 120.
Leygore Farm, 103.
Lillyhorn, 55.
Lincoln, 113.
Lineover Wood, 104.
Little Dean, 33, 113.
Little Dean Camp, 33, 112, 113, 119.
Little Salisbury Camps, 116.
Littleton Camp, 34.
Littleton Drew Barrow, 81.

Littleworth, 3.
Llancaut, 10.
Lodge Park Barrow, 82.
Longborough, 102.
Longhope, 111.
Lower Quinton, 35.
Lugbury, 53, 81.
Luguballium, 119.
Lydbrook, 39.
Lydney, 1, 63, 113, 118, 119.
Lydney Camps, 34, 35.
Lydney Villa, 63, 35, 112.
Lypiatt Park, 105.
Lysons, Rev. S., 26, 58, 59, 65, 68, 85.

M

Maclean, Sir John, 20, 39, 47.
Mangotsfield, 9.
Malvern Hills, 1, 24.
Marlborough, 118.
Marshfield, 9, 25, 34, 49, 107.
Matson, 116.
May Hill, 1, 24.
Meon Hill Camp, 35.
Michaelwood Chase, 17.
Mickleton Parish, 35.
Minchinhampton Parish, 36, 2, 3, 88, 93, 95, 96, 120.
Minsterworth, 119.
Miserden Park, 104.
Mitcheldean Station, 111, 113.
Money Tump, 105.
Monmouth, 113.
Moore, Mr., 56.
Moreton-in-the-Marsh, 4, 27, 114
Moriduuum, 113.

N

Nailsworth, 3, 25, 68, 73, 75, 81, 95 96, 97, 116.
Naunton, 101.
Nettleton, 81.
Newbury, 110.
Newent, 117, 120.
Newmarch, 60, 76.
Newnham, 33, 46, 52, 108, 112, 113.
Niblett, Mr., 62, 65.
Nodons, 64.
Norbury Camp, 37, 94, 103, 114.
North Stoke Village, 30, 107.
Northleach, 37, 44, 53, 73, 77, 79, 82, 94, 114, 117.
North Cerney, 38, 3, 120.
Nose Hill Barrow, 101.
Notgrove Barrow, 82.
Nottingham Hill Camp, 38.
Nympsfield Barrow, 83, 82.

O

Oakle Street, 115.
Oakley Park, 60.
Oddington, 102.
Offa's Dyke, 38, 5, 10.
Offa, King, 10, 38, 49.
Oldbury Camps, 39.
Oldbury Court Camp, 40.
Oldbury Parish, 39, 106, 107, 120.
Oven, The, 96.

Over Park, 107.
Oxenton Hill Camp, 40 53 104
Oxenton Parish, 40.

P

Painswick, 16, 28, 54, 64
Painswick Beacon, 28.
Painswick Villa, 64.
Patch Way, 116.
Pegler's Knobb, 102.
Perrott's Brook, 3.
Penpole Point, 2.
Pen Wood, 45.
Picked Morden, 102.
Piercefield Park, 119.
Pig Street, 120.
Pinbury Camp, 40, 78.
Playne, Mr., 3, 5, 7, 10, 17, 25, 29, 31, 35, 42, 45, 47, 49.
Popes Wood, 80.
Port Way, 116, 120.
Portus Felix, 113.
Prestbury, 12, 13, 41.
Prestbury Earthworks, 41.
Preston, 111.
Prinknash Park, 15, 16, 80, 116.
Puckham Camp, 41.
Puesdown, 114.
Purnell, Mr., 65.

Q

Querns, 76.

R

Ranbury Camp, 42.
Randwick Barrow, 84.
Randwick Camp, 42, 106.
Ratæ, 113.
Redhill Grove, 39.
Rendcomb, 104.
Ridge Way, 116, 1, 110.
Rissington, Little, 103.
Robin's Wood Hill, 24.
Rodborough, 115.
Rodborough Camp, 42.
Rodmarton Barrow, 85.
Rodmarton Villa, 64.
Rodmarton Parish, 58, 64, 65, 115.
Rolleston, Professor, 90, 100, 101.
Rollwright, 11.
Ross, 111, 116, 117.
Rossley, 18.
Rownham Hill Camp, 47.
Royce, Rev. D., 86.
Rudder, 4, 10, 14, 21, 29, 30, 38, 40, 43, 44, 48.
Ryknield Street, 116, 109.

S

Saintbury Camp, 43, 52, 100, 109.
Salinæ, 119.
Salmonsbury, 43, 14, 36, 37, 44, 110, 114.
Salperton, 44, 103, 117.
Salperton Camp, 44, 103.
Salt Way, 117, 45, 77, 79, 103, 114.
Sapperton, 21.

Sarendells, 66.
Sarn Way, 117, 67, 114.
Scarborough Farm, 101.
Scrubditch Farm, 3.
Sea Mills, 2, 110, 119.
Seaton, 113.
Sedbury Park, 39.
Sedgebarrow, 116, 117.
Selsley Camp, 45.
Selsley Hill, 24.
Selsley Hill Barrow, 85.
Sevenhampton, 41, 70, 104.
Severn River, 1, 2, 4, 15, 21, 24, 30, 35, 39, 111, 115, 117, 118, 119.
Severn Valley, 9, 31, 42.
Sherborne, 82.
Sherston, 45.
Shipton Olive, 26, 114.
Shurdington, 77, 114.
Siddington, 111.
Silchester, 118.
Silures, 30, 52.
Sodbury Camp, 46, 61, 107, 116.
Sodbury, Chipping, 19, 27, 46, 61, 120.
Soundborough Farm, 104.
Sowdley Camp, 46, 119.
Speech House, 112.
Speen, 110.
Sponebed Hill, 120.
Spoonley Villa, 70.
Spriggswell, 3.
Stancombe, 65.
Standish Park, 105.
Stanton Drew, 49.
Stantway, 119.
Stapleton Parish, 40.
Stinchcombe Hill, 1, 24.
Stinchcombe Parish, 19.
Stinchcombe Villa, 65.
Stonefield, 115.
Stokeleigh Camps, 47, 14.
Stow-on-the-Wold, 15, 21, 27, 28, 51, 65, 78, 102, 103, 110, 120.
Stow Green Camp, 47.
Stratford-on-Avon, 35.
Stratton, 111.
Stroud, 36, 42, 45, 50, 55, 56, 68, 75, 84, 85, 93, 95, 97, 107, 116.
St. Vincent's Rocks, 13.
Sudeley, 66, 70.
Sutton Coldfield, 116
Swainswick, 116.
Swell Barrows, 86, 87, 101.
Swell Lower Parish, 65, 101, 102.
Swell Upper Parish, 102.
Swell Villa, 65, 114.
Symonds Hall Hill, 106, 115.
Symonds Yat, 47.

T

Taylor, Isaac, 117.
Temple Guiting, 101.
Tetbury, 45, 81, 115.
Tetbury Camp, 48.
Tewkesbury, 24, 49, 116, 117, 119.
Thornbury, 39, 108, 116, 120.
Thornbury, Rev. N., 74.
Througham Barrow, 87.
Tibbs Cross, 112.
Tiddenham, 10, 14, 54, 108, 119.

Tinglestone Barrow, 88.
Tintern Abbey, 39.
Toddington Camp, 48.
Tog Hill Camp, 49, 22.
Tormarton, 107, 116.
Tortworth Park, 7, 59.
Towbury Camp, 49.
Tracey Park, 49.
Trajectus, 49, 6, 118.
Trewsbury Camp, 50, 114, 115.
Turkdean, 103.
Twining, 49.
Tyne, 116.
Tytherington Camp, 121, 115.

U

Uley Bury, 50.
Uley Barrow, 88, 82, 84.
Upper Slaughter, 51, 20, 103, 120.
Upton St. Leonards, 116.
Uxella, 119.

V

Venta Silurum, 6, 15, 115, 118.
Via Julia, 118, 112, 113, 115, 116, 119, 120.
Via Regia, 66, 110, 120.

W

Wadfield Villa, 66.
Wagborough, 103, 109.
Wall, 116.
Wansdyke, 13.
Waste Tumulus, 108.
Watling Street, 116.
Welshbury, 52, 34, 112, 113.
Westbury-on-Severn, 113, 119.
Weston Park, 2
Weston Subedge, 109.
Western Trackway, 119, 110, 120.
Westridge Hill, 6.
West Tump, 89, 87.
White Way, 120. 16, 38.
Whitfield Tump, 93.
Whittington, 26, 69.
Winchcombe, 4, 11, 48, 66, 70, 74.
Windmill Tump, 85.
Windrush Camp, 53.
Windrush River, 51, 56.
Wilcote, 115.
Willersey Barrow, 93.
Willersey Camp, 52, 43, 109.
Winterbourne, 9.
Witcomb, 66, 16, 60, 111, 117.
Withington Barrow, 94.
Withington Villa, 67, 68, 120.
Wolston Camp, 53.
Woodbury, 53.
Woodchester Villa, 68, 116.
Wyck Beacon, 103.
Wycomb, 69, 18, 70, 114, 120.

Y

Yewbury Camp, 54.

www.ingramcontent.com/pod-product-compliance
Lightning Source LLC
Chambersburg PA
CBHW021800230426
43669CB00006B/143